CREE NARRATIVE MEMORY

FROM TREATIES TO CONTEMPORARY TIMES

Neal McLeod

PURICH
PUBLISHING
LIMITED
SASKATOON, SK. CANADA

Purich Publishing Ltd.
Box 23032, Market Mall Post Office, Saskatoon, SK, Canada, S7J 5H3
Phone: (306) 373-5311 Fax: (306) 373-5315 Email: purich@sasktel.net
Website: www.purichpublishing.com

Library and Archives Canada Cataloguing in Publication

McLeod, Neal
    Cree narrative memory: from treaties to contemporary times / Neal McLeod.

Includes bibliographical references and index.
ISBN 978-1-895830-31-6

1. Cree Indians – Saskatchewan – Historiography. 2. Cree Indians – Saskatchewan – History. 3. Cree Indians – Saskatchewan – Folklore. 4. Cree Indians – Saskatchewan – Ethnic identity. 5. Oral tradition – Saskatchewan. 6. Oral tradition – Prairie Provinces. 7. Storytelling – Saskatchewan. 8. Oral history – Saskatchewan. I. Title.

E99.C88M35 2007   971.24004'97323   C2007-904396-8

Cover design by Duncan Campbell.
Cover image of Grandmother and *wîhtikôhkân* courtesy Grace Vandall.
Cover painting by Larry Jacobsen / iStockphoto.
Editing, design, layout, and map by Donald Ward.
Cree editing by Arok Wolvengrey.
Index by Ursula Acton.
Printed and bound in Canada by Houghton Boston Printers *&* Lithographers, Saskatoon.

Purich Publishing gratefully acknowledges the assistance of the Government of Canada through the Canada Book Fund, and the Creative Industry Growth and Sustainability Program made possible through funding provided to the Saskatchewan Arts Board by the Government of Saskatchewan through the Ministry of Parks, Culture, and Sport for its publishing program.

Printed on 100 per cent post-consumer, recycled, ancient-forest-friendly paper.

 Canadian Patrimoine Heritage canadien

 Saskatchewan Ministry of Tourism, Parks, Culture and Sport

 SASKATCHEWAN ARTS BOARD

CONTENTS

Note to Readers

Cree names and terminology are used extensively throughout this book. For readers unfamiliar with Cree, a complete glossary appears on page 101.

ACKNOWLEDGEMENTS

THERE ARE MANY PEOPLE I would like to thank for their inspiration and help in the writing of this book.

First and foremost, I would like to thank my father, Jerry McLeod, and my uncle, Burton Vandall, for giving me a solid grounding in Cree stories as I was growing up. My great-grandfather *kôkôcîs*, Peter Vandall, was my strongest link to the past, and I would like to thank his memory and his spirit for giving me the chance to know stories that stretch generations back from my own time and place.

My grandparents, John R. McLeod and Ida McLeod, also played a key role in shaping me and giving me a sensitivity for recognizing the importance of our ancestral narrative heritage and the importance and power of language.

I would also like to thank many other people, including: *cîhcam; kwêcic;* Big John Janvier; *wîhtikôhkân; asiniy-kâpaw;* Gabriel Vandall; the late Beatrice Lavallee; Isadore Pelletier; Charlie Burns; Clifford Sanderson; Abel and Maggie McLeod; my children, Cody, Ally, Jordan, Justin, and Glen; my wife, Christine; my former students, Melissa Blind and "Tina" Hannah-Munns; and my colleagues, Arok Wolvengrey, Winona Wheeler, Blair Stonechild, Robert Nestor, David Miller, and David Newhouse. I would also like to thank Grant Kernan for restoring some key family photographs.

I thank Maria Campbell, Louise Halfe, and Norval Morrisseau whose work inspired me and grounded me in the importance of narratives, language, and story. I also thank Purich Publishing for believing in the book and bringing it to press, and Don Ward for doing a beautiful job (once again) with typesetting and design.

The greatest Cree storytellers often said, "*môya mistahi ê-kiskêyihtamân* (I do not know much)." I would have to say, "*nama kîkway ê-kiskêyihtamân* (I know nothing)"; the truths that resonate from the pages of this book are not mine, but the echoes of ancient voices that I have imperfectly articulated.

Without our great storytellers and our political leaders, such as *mistahi-maskwa* and John Tootoosis, we would be lost in a dominant culture's language and memory. It is to our Old Men and Old Women that we owe our greatest thanks.

INTRODUCTION

As the late Lakota writer Vine Deloria, Jr. noted, Indigenous people tend to envision their collective memory in terms of space rather than time.[1] It is the sense of place that anchors our stories; it is the sense of place that links us together as communities. Indeed, it is the sense of space that connects us to other beings and the rest of creation.

The connection Indigenous people have to the land is housed in language. Through stories and words, we hold the echo of generational experience, and the engagement with land and territory. *nêhiyawêwin*, Cree language — perhaps more poetically rendered as "the process of making Cree sound" — grounds us, and binds us with other living beings, and marks these relationships.

The "echo" metaphor has often been used by Cree storytellers as a way of describing the past coming up to the present through stories. The late Jim Kâ-Nîpitêhtêw, an elder from Onion Lake, said that what he knew was like an "echo of older voices from a long time ago."[2] Once, when Edwin Tootoosis was visiting my father, he told me, "*môy ê-kistawêt*" ("It does not echo"). He was referring to the land, and the fact that the land no longer had sound in the same way it had before.

I have heard stories of a great deer that lived by a hill near Prince Albert. This deer was able to hear for a long distance. As the landscape was changing, with the coming of newcomers, the deer, with this exceptional capacity to hear, retreated into the earth.

With the coming of newcomers to the territory of the Cree, the landscape was transformed as well through a naming process. *kistapinânihk* became Prince Albert. Regina, named for the Queen, is known as *oskana kâ-asastêki* (pile of bones) in Cree; instead of celebrating the empire, the name was a marker for the retreat of the buffalo from the land. Today, the road maps of western Canada show little evidence that Indigenous people dwell in the territory, or that we have marked the place with our memory.

My strongest narrative link to the past is through my father, Jerry McLeod, from the James Smith Reserve (*nihtâwikihcikanisihk*) in east central Saskatchewan. He, in turn, was told many stories by his grandfather, Peter Vandall (*kôkôcîs*), from the Sandy Lake Reserve. *kôkôcîs* had been told many stories by his grandfather, *wîhtikôhkân*. These stories and others inform me about who I am. They explore the various aspects of my existence, and form the fabric of my being.

The foundation of this book lies in the memories of my grandparents and great-grandparents, whose life experiences reach into the memories of those who came before them, the Ancient Ones. And, of course, the words and narratives of others who have taken the time to share them with me help make up this book.

Cree narrative memory is more than simply storytelling. A skilled storyteller strings narratives together to suit a particular audience. Some details may be downplayed or accentuated, depending on what the occasion calls for. As the storyteller weaves his tale, there are elements of description and analysis: the storyteller describes events and experiences, but also analyzes this

The buffalo played a central role in the life of the *nêhiyawak* (Saskatchewan Archives Board, R-A21969).

experience. The stories are reflected upon and critically examined, and they are brought to life by being integrated into the experience of the storyteller and the audience.

This book, which I have called *Cree Narrative Memory*, captures only parts of the larger collective memory. No story is complete in itself. Anyone who attempts to link various pieces of stories together into a larger story is always limited. There are always details of stories which we may not know and which we will learn in time. Even our understanding of narratives is incomplete at any given moment. The perspectives and vantage points are as unlimited as experience itself.

With limits to our understanding of narratives also come limits in terms of the stories passed on to us. Some of the details of narratives are not readily known; there are, at times, small holes, lost details, in the collective memory. One such hole is the name of the wife of *wîhtikôhkân* (who is pictured on the cover), the mother of Big John and Virginia.

While I do not know her name, I acknowledge her importance to the process of storytelling and life in my family. If she did not exist, I would not exist. While I know few details of her life, I know of her indirectly through the stories of Big John, *kôkôcîs*, and others. In fact, she is like the wind: I cannot see her directly in the stories, but I can see her influence in the life and stories of others. Like the wind, we see her indirectly in the movements of other beings.

Cree narrative memory is a large, intergenerational, collective memory. Cree narratives form part of a larger, collective memory. In Louise Halfe's poetry collection, *Blue Marrow*, there are many insights regarding memory. The opening poem begins: "The walk began before I was a seed. / My mother strung my umbilical cord in my moccasins."[3] This is a Cree practice, but it also metaphorically describes how she carries the memory of the Ancient Ones with her. The walk is the return home through memory after her "memory went to sleep"[4]: the place of storytelling wherein the old people rest. She depicts the collective memory of Cree people as food, essential for the soul:

Grandmothers hold me. I must pass all that I possess,
every morsel to my children. These small gifts
to see them through life. Raise my fist. Tell the story.
Tear down barbed-wire fences.[5]

She sees collective memory as a gift and a responsibility, an intergenerational process. The stories found in memory help people find their way out of colonialism.

Halfe uses another metaphor for memory: "Oh *nôhkomak* [grandmothers], / your Bundles I carry inside."[6] Comprehension of Cree philosophy and worldview is necessary for understanding Cree historical experience. Often, stories are removed from this context. Winona Stevenson uses the metaphor of the "bundle" to describe stories: "The bundle is plundered, the voice silenced, bits are extracted to meet empirical academic needs, and the story dies. In the process, the teachings and responsibilities deriving from the social relations inherent in student-teacher relations are forgotten."[7] A bundle is *nayahcikan*, which means "something you put on your back, something you carry." A bundle is a spiritual embodiment of collective memory and is added to and subtracted from as time goes on. Songs are associated with bundles, and the combination of bundles and songs are passed on within families.

Much of collective memory passes through us through song and prayer. Halfe appeals to her grandmothers, as if in prayer:

pê-nîhtaciwêk, nôhkomak.
Climb down, my Grandmothers.

pê-nânapâcihinân.
Come heal us.

ê-sôhkêpayik kimaskihkîm.
Your medicine so powerful.

kâ-wî-nânapâcihikoyâhk.
That which will heal us.[8]

Part of decolonizing Cree consciousness is for collective narrative memory to be awakened. As Halfe writes, "*nôhkomak* are waking up, / the drum vibrates, / lifts the mass of dawn."[9]

Part of the process of recovering this ancient memory held in sound lies in recording the oral history of our elders while we still have them with us. As a young person in the 1970s, I grew up in the midst of a massive cultural revival in Indigenous communities in Saskatchewan. My grandparents, Ida and John McLeod, were at the forefront of this movement. *nôhkom*, my grandmother, helped to pioneer the standardization of Cree and also the development of a Cree language curriculum. *nimosômipan*, my late grandfather, was chair of the Treaty 6 Centennial Committee and also co-ordinated elders workshops. Both worked for the Saskatchewan Indian Cultural Centre, which was in many ways the beginning of the First Nations University of Canada.

During the 1970s elders workshops at the Saskatchewan Indian Cultural College, Eli Bear from Little Pine reserve noted the importance of the return of Cree memory:

> We are trying to tell people of what was given to us as an Indian nation. We are trying to wake people up, to have respect for our ceremonies and all the Indian ways of life. Because nowadays we seem to hear the elders from a distance; it is as if they are fading away. These elders knew about these medicines and they die without leaving us the way to make these, or where to get them. All these things we don't know about now. But the elders they tried to tell us about these but we didn't listen very hard to them.[10]

Since the 1870s, the Cree people have experienced a great deal of change, often traumatic. It is to these elders of the Cree-speaking people that we owe the survival of our collective soul. In a small way, I have tried to document some of the stories that made my grandparents and other grandparents the people they were. Their passage through the world is a rich pathway that we can all learn from.

To all the grandmothers and grandfathers, I dedicate this book. *hay! hay!*

CHAPTER ONE

CREE NARRATIVE MEMORY

COLLECTIVE MEMORY IS THE ECHO OF OLD STORIES that links grandparents with their grandchildren. In the Cree tradition, collective narrative memory is what puts our singular lives into a larger context. Old voices echo; the ancient poetic memory of our ancestors finds home in our individual lives and allows us to reshape our experience so that we can interpret the world we find ourselves in.

As we find ourselves enmeshed in the trajectories of various stories, we also make contributions to the larger narrative. While we are influenced by the stories of the *kêhtê-ayak* (Old Ones), we also add to the meaning of these stories through our experiences and understanding, and add in small ways to the ancient wisdom.

Narratives are constantly being reinterpreted and recreated in light of shifting experience and context. As Keith Basso has written of Apache stories, they "enrich the common stock on which everyone can draw to muse on past events, interpret their significance, and imagine them now."[1]

Phillip Deloria comments on the dynamic nature of the stories Basso documented: "Apaches . . . do not simply live in a static, mythic world. They create new histories about newly created places, revealing the gaps and fissure in any scheme that would sift out temporal distinctions among native histories."[2]

Richard Preston discusses the importance of narrative in Cree collective memory, stressing its importance in the culture: "Narratives have been the basis for understanding Cree experiences."[3] It is through stories that memory and history are transmitted.

The process of engaging this collective memory involves sitting with elders and storytellers and listening. I remember when I visited Charlie Burns from the James Smith Reserve. He was a friend of my late grandfather, John R. McLeod, and the great-grandson of *iskotêw*, the original Burns. He patiently told stories and helped me find my way through the words. At the end of that day, he gave me a beaded belt and told me that after he had passed away, I would have this belt to remember him and the stories. I was greatly honoured, and felt a profound sense of responsibility as I tried to learn the stories and improve my fluency in the language.

I also was honoured to receive the collection of tapes and papers of my grandparents, Ida and John McLeod. I am the only one of my generation in my family who can converse in Cree, and I feel a deep responsibility in this regard. I would like to continue to gather stories and languages so that the echoes of my ancestors will find some embodiment in the present.

The sense of responsibility in Cree narrative memory is embodied in the way Cree *kêhtê-ayak* used to address young people. Sometimes they would stick a knife in the ground and say, "If what I say angers you, you can use this knife on me" — or there might be a variation on this, such as, "If you do not believe what I say, you can use this knife on me."

There are various ways by which one can understand the use of the knife in the storytelling tradition of the Crees. The first component of this powerful symbolism is the relationship that the person speaking, the storyteller, has with those who are listening. The connection might be kinship or friendship, but there would be a relationship. The second component is the knife, a powerful symbol: if the younger person did not listen, it would be like a knife that would kill both the story and the storyteller.

wâhkôhtowin (Kinship) and Narrative Memory

I understand Cree narrative memory through the stories I have heard and the relationships that sustain them. My interest in Cree memory would not have been possible if my father had not raised me and if I had not had the grandparents I had. My grandfather devoted his life to the betterment of Indian people's lives through education; my grandmother devoted her life to reviving the Cree language through the development of a standard orthography, as well as the creation of educational materials.

In constructing my sense of the world, I have drawn upon memories and narratives. I remember one particular day very clearly, going to Thunderchild reserve (*kâ-pitihkonâhk*) near North Battleford, Saskatchewan, with *nimosôm*. There was a large gathering of old people. They were all sitting in a circle, smoking a pipe, and they got up and took turns talking. At my grandfather's funeral the old people also sat in a circle and smoked the pipe; "Old Jim" (Jim Kâ-Nîpitêhtêw) performed that ceremony. I will always remember these things, and the knowledge held in the words and actions of the old ones in their struggle to maintain their *nêhiyâwiwin* (Cree-ness) in the face of Anglo-Canadian culture. I was also struck by the realization that I was part of a collective memory much larger than myself.

nimosôm struggled to find a balance in his life narratives between the old ways and the new. Noel Dyck, a long-time friend of my grandfather, noted that it was the stories of his life and those he had heard from his grandmother *kêhkêhk-iskwêw* (Hawk Woman, Betsy McLeod, born in 1866) that he drew on in "his public acts of remembering."[4] This concept of remembering publicly is important because it gets to the heart of Cree narrative history. These storytellers remembered because they felt a moral duty to do so. Stories were offered as traces of experience through which the listeners had to make sense of their own lives and experiences. My grandfather told stories about what he knew; he derived his stories from his experience, and he told stories in which he, or his ancestors, were participants.

Knowledge within this paradigm of knowing comes from what you have seen and what you have internalized. Noel Dyck writes that my grandfather "began telling his listeners that since he had only a grade three education he could only speak about things that had happened to him, things that he knew about."[5] Dyck called this approach a "traditional Cree *genre*."[6] A fundamental aspect of this approach is open-endedness. My grandfather "never said what the points of his stories were; he forced the listeners to discover this for themselves."[7] Consequently, people make up their own minds about what they think about something; they have to decide what they believe to be true and the listener is given a chance to internalize the stories.

My understanding of Cree narrative memory was also nourished by my late great-grandfather, Peter Vandall (*kôkôcîs*), who died when I was fourteen. He was raised by his grandfather, *wîhtikôhkân*, an old hunter from the bush country in northern Alberta. I remember the sound of *kôkôcîs*'s voice and the smell of his Copenhagen chewing tobacco. His stories are perhaps my strongest link to the past. He spoke of *nêhiyâwiwin* (Cree-ness) with a fluidity and humour that could only come from one who saw great joy in life and was comfortable with who he was.

A variety of factors led me to be close to this old man. One was owing to Cree socio-linguistic etiquette. Within Cree culture, communication between a man and his mother-in-law, and between a woman and her father-in-law, was frowned upon. My grandmother, Ida McLeod (née Vandall), would not have been allowed to talk to her father-in-law, Abel McLeod. She actually talked to him only twice: once it involved politics, and I do not know the circumstances of the other interaction. There are stories that emphasize this taboo against speaking to in-laws. When a wife was in labour, for instance, the husband went to his mother-in-law's house and had to convey the message to a cat in the room; that is, he had to talk to the cat.

Another reason I was close to this old man was my resemblance to *wîhtikôhkân*, his grandfather: my great-grandfather, *kôkôcîs,* said that I had the same *presence* as his grandfather, including his eyes. Perhaps, for *kôkôcîs, wîhcikôs* (the diminutive of *wîhtikôhkân*), I was the link to the past that *kôkôcîs* was for me. I was always close to this old man, and I remember the five-dollar bills he would give me when I visited him in the warm days of spring and summer.

Kinship, *wâhkôhtowin*, grounds the collective narrative memory within *nêhiyâwiwin*. There are important relationships not only among human beings, but also with the rest of creation. *wîsahkêcâhk*, the elder brother (mistakenly called the "trickster" by many), is perhaps the most vibrant demonstration of the importance of relationships and the fluid line between humans and animals. *wâhkôhtowin* keeps narrative memory grounded and

kôkôcîs, Peter Vandall
(courtesy Grace Vandall).

embedded within an individual's life stories. It also grounds the transmission of Cree narrative memory: people tell stories to other people who are part of the stories and who assume the moral responsibility to remember.

I remember the stories of *nicâpân* (Betsy Head, my great-grandmother's sister) during a visit I paid to her in the spring of 1998. I sat with her for a day and listened. She told me stories, including one about my namesake, *nîkân-isi* ("the one who comes first," Thunderbird), who was also known by his everyday name of *mahkiyoc* ("the big one"). That is where we got the name McLeod: a Scottish missionary who was handing out names thought that *mahkiyoc* sounded like McLeod. *nîkân-isi* was a Saulteaux who came from near Lake Winnipegosis[8]; however, two of his brothers went southwest to join Chief Little Pine's people because they did not want to take treaty at the James Smith Reserve. Undoubtedly I understood these narratives differently than *nicâpân* did, but we were bound together through a common collective narrative process.

These stories, and parts of them, emerged when I sat with *nicâpân*. She asked me to record the words. I sat in her kitchen; the floor had worn patches on it, paths where she had walked. I thought of those paths as metaphors for her journey through life. They were like the pathways of memory, maps of where she had been. They represented how she had travelled, the connection with the land.

I thought about how much information she had. She had lived a rich life and always tried to be a good human being. Her life was not merely a series of scratches on paper; her stories were like an organism, a living thing that linked stories and experience together. She told me about my great-great-great grandfather, Bernard Constant, who had put his name to Treaty 6 in 1876 as a band counsellor of the James Smith band. She told me what life was like when she was younger; the happiness she remembered lingered in her words. She had lived a long time, but there was still a lightness and ease in her. She was very open with her stories, and her age gave her authority. Her stories were a map that helped me find my place in the world.

The Reliability of Collective Narrative Memory

Life experience shows the dynamic nature of Cree narrative memory, which could be conceived of as an organism growing and shifting. Nonetheless, like all organisms, Cree narrative memory has a structure within the parameters of possibility, and there is a great deal of stability.

The prodigious memory of Jim Kâ-Nîpitêhtêw, the fact that he could re-cite the stories of old people directly, illustrates the stability of oral tradition. The narrative of the treaty coalesced through the discussion of several old men (including Kâ-Nîpitêhtêw's father and paternal uncle); it would include sections of the "The Pipestem and the Making of Treaty 6": [3], [5], [6], [7], [8], [14], and [15].[9] All these accounts that document the treaty signed at Fort Pitt in 1876 demonstrate the reliability of the treaty narrative.

Listeners or readers must also acknowledge the humility that old people have in Cree narrative. While there may be oral narratives that are very close to the original, old people hesitate to claim that they know one completely. Many begin with "*namôya mistahi ê-kiskêyihtamân*" ("I do not know very much").

This simple phrase is important in understanding Cree narrative memory. People did not believe they had power over the narrative, or owned it; rather, they believed that they were conduits, that there was a balance between the individual and tradition. When the play between individual and collective is taken into account, it becomes evident that no understanding can ever be complete, because there could always be more interpretations. Paul Ricoeur's notion of a "surplus of meaning" complements this point.

An example of the humility found within Cree narrative is Jim Kâ-Nîpitêhtêw's discussion of Treaty 6. He wonders whether he remembers things well enough: "*â, êwako ôma kâ-wî-tâhkôtamân, matwân cî kwayask nika-kî-isi-tâhkôtên tânis ê-kî-itâcimostawit kâ-kî-oyôhtâwîyân*"[10] ("Well, this which I am about to discuss, I wonder if I will be able to discuss it with proper faithfulness, just as my father had told me").[11]

Another point must be made: statements such as the one above also act as "oral footnotes." In written cultures, we document where we obtain ideas through a bibliography; in oral cultures, "footnoting" is done by acknowledging how one came to know a story.

In another example, Walter Lightning discusses his work with various Cree old people in his article "Compassionate Mind: Implications of a Text Written by Elder Louis Sunchild." Lightning discusses the importance of humility in terms of collective memory:

I said to him [Art Rainy Bird from Montana] in Cree, "Grandfather, I don't know how to do these things. I am trying to prepare the protocol but I realize that basically I don't know anything. As a matter of fact, I have no idea what I'm doing. Please, I implore you, have compassion for what I am doing."[12]

Lightning is conscious of the limitations of his knowledge of *nêhiyâwiwin* and feels humble before the older man. The old man reciprocates by acknowledging his own limitations. Lightning continues the dialogue: "Elder Art Bird, for all his stature and knowledge, was a living example of humility. He looked at me and answered with a deep kindness of understanding, saying, 'It's nothing, my grandson. We don't know anything'."[13]

Underlying this conversation is the respect these men have for the larger collective knowledge of their people: neither claims to possess great knowledge. Humility is a primary characteristic of Cree narrative memory and acknowledges that narratives are open-ended. There is no end to how they can be interpreted.

There is another way in which oral traditions can be considered open-ended: different elements of a story can be emphasized during a single performance, which can be characterized as the occasion of telling. In other words, there can never be a "complete" authoritative performance of a narrative because the audience and the demands of the occasion will always vary. Furthermore, a narrative can never be exhausted, because the dynamics between the teller and the listener will also vary. The story will always be understood in slightly different ways, depending on the experiences of the people listening.

Toward a Notion of Spiritual History / *âtayôhkêwina*

Within the Cree language, there are several insights that allow us to construct what we might call "spiritual history." The term for the narratives of the elder brother (*wîsahkêcâhk*) is *âtayôhkêwina*. The term can also apply to other narratives involving spiritual beings which are described as *âtayôhkanak*, which means "spiritual helpers," spiritual grandfathers and grandmothers. These narratives are essential because they give insight into the way in which Cree people related to their ecology and the environment, and with other beings.

If one wants to understand the narrative memory of Cree people, one has to look at it through the lens of Indigenous knowing and of the cultural forces that shaped the stories in the first place. The notion of "spiritual history" simply urges us to try to engage the narratives through the lens of those who originally experienced it.

The notion of "spiritual history" challenges the Western notion of the construction of linear time. Various beings exist throughout long stretches of time, and their relationship to Cree people is constructed more along the lines of a relationship to space and location rather than linear time.

Cree narratives are held within oral traditions and social relationships and provide a counterpoint to the narratives of non-Cree society. The activity and process of these narratives challenge the hegemony of the mainstream discourse, which has often been conflated with notions of "progress" that have ultimately undermined Cree narrative memory and been used as a tool of conquest. Cree narratives have often been relegated to a lower status because of Western historical conventions. Such beliefs are often dismissed as "mythology" and pre-historical within the confines of mainstream historiography. As Maori scholar Linda Smith notes:

> In order for history to begin there has to be a period of beginning and some criteria for determining when something begins. In terms of history this was often attached to concepts of "discovery," the development of literacy, or the development of specific social formation. Everything before that time is designated as prehistorical, belonging to the realm of myths and traditions, "outside" the domain.[14]

Colonial powers, mainstream historians, and academics have often thought of Indigenous "lived" memory as myth. Even among historians sympathetic to Cree narratives, there is still a bias against Cree spirituality. An example can be found in David Meyer's history of the Red Earth Cree, a community to the northeast of *nihtâwikihcikanisihk* (the James Smith Reserve):

> Of course, by academic standards, Wihciko's [sic] narrative does not appear to be entirely historical, or wholly secular. However, it is apparent that in the Cree frame of reference accounts of Wihtiko [sic] encounters and magical happenings are considered historical. As far as these people are concerned, these events did occur; they were marvelous and important occurrences and therefore are recalled in the oral history.[15]

In fairness to Meyer, he examines the historicity of the Red Earth narratives in Cree people's perspectives. These narratives are not situated in relation to other historiographic approaches, apart from a mild skepticism.

Cree narrative memory emerges from the worldview and spirituality of the Cree people, and is grounded in the names of both ancestors and places. It is through our connections to storytellers and *kêhtê-ayak* that we are able to access this ancient collective memory. Cree narrative memory is ongoing, and is sustained through relationships, respect, and responsibility.

CHAPTER TWO

CREE NARRATIVES OF PLACE

IN ADDITION TO BEING AN INTERGENERATIONAL PROCESS, Cree collective memory is anchored in places and landscape. The various place-names within Cree narrative form the basis for a shorthand encoding of experience, of various relationships, and the articulation of core Cree values and worldviews.

Indigenous people remain attached to an area of land over an extended period of time. This connection is manifested through such things as the knowledge of plants, sacred sites, and songs. Indigenous people remain attached to specific pieces of land, shown through songs, ceremonies, and language.

mistasiniy

Over the years I heard stories of "big stones," *mistasiniyak*, commonly called grandfathers. These grandfather stones were key markers in the landscape and important places for Indigenous people to have ceremonies and pray.

Isadore Pelletier, an elder at First Nations University of Canada, talked about stones north of Regina:

I never counted how many stones were there, but it's fairly big, a circle, it [is] about a hundred by a hundred around. . . . If they had a problem within their group, they would go to that place and have a talking circle or if they met up with another tribe of people, that's where they would go and talk and smoke their pipes.[1]

Pelletier went on to say:

> The stones, as you probably know, are listeners, they are grandfathers, they are older than, you know, just as old as Mother Earth . . . and that's why we call them grandfathers . . . there was a reason why they put them, they're all spaced equally all around, and the significance of that is when the person spoke, when he got up and spoke, and they spoke, they spoke the truth . . . there was . . . no lies told when they spoke there. . . .[2]

I heard a story from La Ronge, a community in northern Saskatchewan, of how missionaries took a grandfather stone to the middle of the lake in winter so that it would fall to the bottom of the lake on break-up. Part of the process of Christianization involved the erasing of a previous Cree memory which had been marked in the landscape by sacred stones.

One important place in the landscape of Cree traditional territory in western Canada is a place at the western tip of the Qu'Appelle Valley (*kâ-têpwêwi-sîpiy*) called *mistasiniy*. Many years ago, my father mentioned a stone there called *mistasiniy*. He related how people used to come there, leave offerings, and pray. He described the stone as being hollow.

mistasiniy became a place where people would gather and pray, to honour

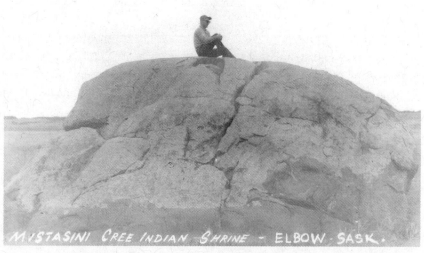

mistasiniy (Saskatchewan Archives Board, R-DQ Album No. 8 #4).

the buffalo who sustained them. They would leave gifts of thankfulness, such as tobacco and *wêpinâson*, to thank the Creator and the Grandfather Buffalo for the gifts that had been bestowed upon them. Pelletier discussed the importance of the rock:

> . . . that stone that was at Diefenbaker Lake, there must have been a place where people congregated, and whenever they went by there they made a special . . . detour to go put offerings down for that . . . stone, and people would even . . . lay on that stone to get healed and that's one good things that those stones were used for.[3]

This has also been noted by others, such as Henry Youle Hind who moved through the area in an expedition in the 1850s.

This stone was destroyed in 1966 when the Qu'Appelle River was connected to the South Saskatchewan River and the Gardiner Dam was built. The land where the stone rested was to be flooded, so it was thought that parts of the stone should be salvaged and used to construct a cairn.

Ironically, the lake created by the dam was named after John Diefenbaker, the conservative Prime Minister from Prince Albert. Diefenbaker is still held in high regard among older Cree people for the way he championed the rights of Indigenous people. He often represented Indigenous people in court, took the time to visit with them on the streets of Prince Albert, and passionately defended the dignity of all human beings.

In a strange turn of history, then, the site that marks the destruction of Grandfather Buffalo acquires the name of Diefenbaker who, metaphorically like Grandfather Buffalo, wanted to care for the weakest and most powerless in society — the Indigenous people of the prairies.

With this change of names and the destruction of the stone, there came a concurrent shift of names and memory. While many people thought the stone could be saved, engineers said it was hollow and would not remain intact if it were moved. In 1967, the remnants of the stone were made into a cairn.

The grandfather stone called *mistasiniy* is spoken of in the story *paskwâw-mostos awâsis*, Buffalo Child. I will go through the story with specific reference to the version spoken in the *kâ-têpwêwi-sîpiy* Valley, but I will also reference variations of the story in Cree-speaking territory.

Stan Cuthand, a noted storyteller from Little Pine Reserve in Saskatchewan, told the story of *mistasiniy* in the Qu'Appelle Valley in 1977:

A long time ago a small band of Crees were crossing the prairies. An old lady was with them, and with her there was a small child, a boy. She was leading a big dog on a leash, and the dog was pulling the child in a travois. All of a sudden the old lady lost her hold on the leash, and the dog ran off to chase the Buffalo.[4]

The story told by Henry Cardinal, from the Saddle Lake Reserve in Alberta, references a spot in the landscape of Alberta called "where the prairie ends."[5] Cardinal describes the feelings of the boy on being separated from his grandmother: "The children would ride a travois which was pulled by a dog. He was lost when he fell from the travois. The small children would cry and the buffalo heard them cry'."[6]

Cuthand adds:

The Buffalo stampeded. She lost the child. The dog went for miles and miles chasing the Buffalo until he stopped to drink from a water hole. There were no wheels on the travois, just two sticks. These got stuck and the dog crawled out of his harness, leaving the child behind in the carryall. The dog came home but the child was never found.

In the meadow there were two bachelors, an old bull and a young bull — we speak of Buffalo as if they were people — and as they grazed around they heard the child crying. "You know, I feel sorry for this child. Let's raise him up as one of our own."[7]

The other bull, however, did not want to raise the child; he said that the boy's people tried to kill the buffalo. The old buffalo was named *nikisêyiniwikwêmês* (Old Man Buffalo),[8] and he settled the conflict by saying that the winner of a race would decide the fate of the boy. The older buffalo then won the race and raised and protected the boy.

An old lady asked the medicine man to have a shaking tent, an important ceremony of the Cree, to learn the location of the boy. They then travelled down the *kâ-têpwêwi-sîpiy* (Qu'Appelle River Valley):

"We will find him," they all said. All of a sudden they came upon a great rock shaped like a bull Buffalo. "That's the one! That's the one!" They all camped there, having the pipe ceremony and leaving gifts and offerings to the spirit of the lodge.[9]

A parallel story seems to have its roots in the general area of the Qu'Appelle Valley and is found in the narratives of Gabriel Crow Buffalo,[10] who is from the Daystar Reserve, roughly 120 km north of Regina. In the version told by Gabriel Crow Buffalo, the boy is told eventually that it is time to go home. Spiritually gifted people knew that he was coming back and prepared an area for his return.

Another storyteller, Alexander Wolfe, from the Sakimay Reserve along the Qu'Appelle River, noted in his version that two orphaned children are separated from their tribe. After being taken care of by the grandfather buffalo, they go back to their people and are eventually respected as leaders.[11]

The boy had the ability to change physical form (*ê-kwêskîmot*). In the version told by Stan Cuthand[12] and Barry Ahenakew,[13] the grandfather eventually told the buffalo boy that he was not part of the buffalo, that he was from the people that chased them (the hunters). Buffalo Child, *paskwâw-mostos awâsis*, sees his reflection and knows this to be true.[14] Eventually, the Crees pursue them and his father pleads with him to flee to save his life; he was in human form then[15] and "rolled four times" to become a buffalo. While the Cree hunters watch, he transforms himself into a stone, "but not the same size he had been as a bull. He was much bigger than a rock and seemed to grow. These Cree hunters were amazed. The buffalo-shaped rock grew to such a tremendous size, it looked like a buffalo sitting down. It was a buffalo sitting down."[16]

In all the versions, Grandfather Buffalo tells the young man, "I will provide for you." The stone was a physical reminder of the relationship between people and the rest of creation, particularly the buffalo. But the stone was also a concrete reminder of some of the most treasured values of Cree culture, such as the attempt to care for those who have no one to provide for them. In all the versions, kinship is stressed, and also the importance of taking care of orphans.

The narrative shared by Henry Cardinal links the story of the buffalo boy to the creation of the buffalo pound. Buffalo Boy is referred to as someone who had this inner power.[17] Tobacco was given to him to help his people get buffalo to eat. He then teaches the people how to make a corral:

> Then they were made of fences and they had to be very high in order to contain the buffalo. If they are low the buffalo just jumped over them with no difficulty. The first buffalo pound was built almost like a bridge and once the buffalo crossed there was no way they could turn back,

that is when they used the bow and arrow for them. After that time this man [Buffalo Boy] was responsible for showing others how to make the buffalo jumping pounds.[18]

It is interesting to note that there is also a sacred story of *wîsahkêcâhk* regarding the creation of the buffalo pound.

Isadore Pelletier's narrative about a stone in Hudson Bay shows us that there were other stones throughout the landscape that connected us to the power of the land:

> There is another stone down by Hudson's Bay, and I remember, I recall my mother talking about this. This stone, it was real, it was a real, big, big, big stone. And she said it was so heavy that it kind of caved. . . . But she said when you went there, there was beaded moccasins, there was guns, there was stuff that was left there, you know, for offering for that stone.[19]

All these stones are called Grandfathers, and show our kinship to the territory.

Other Important Places

There is another significant point in the landscape of Cree-speaking people: *kâ-pitihkonâhk*, which got its name from *nipiy kâ-pitihkwêk,* meaning "Sounding Lake." Sounding Lake in eastern Alberta is where Thunderchild's people entered into Treaty 6 in 1879.

When I was a child, I went with my grandfather to *kâ-pitihkonâhk* (the Thunderchild Reserve) near North Battleford. There was a gathering to discuss treaties and other traditional narratives. The old people spoke Cree and smoked a pipe and narratives of *kêhtê-ayak* were collected and recorded.

Eventually, Thunderchild's band came to settle near the town of Delmas, Saskatchewan, but the people retained the reference to Sounding Lake where they had spent so much time before the reserve period. Thus, the name for the reserve means "The Land of the Sounding Lake People." Many of the old people who gathered that day at Thunderchild were only a generation removed from the old way of life, and spoke stories thick with echoes. They understood the power of language to carry a people and hold a place in the world.

The old people from the Land of Sounding Lake people had threads of memory from the time of *mistahi-maskwa* (Big Bear). *piyêsiw-awâsis* (Thunderchild) had been close to *mistahi-maskwa*; so, too, was the father of my *mosôm's* (my grandfather's) mentor, Jim Kâ-Nîpitêhtêw. His father had been beside *mistahi-maskwa* during the 1885 troubles.

nipiy kâ-pitihkwêk, the source of the name *kâ-pitihkonâhk*, comes from an old story about a thunderbird that was dragged into the water by a snake. Stories about thunderbirds and snakes are common among Cree people. The water of the lake was rumbling, full of sound, of echoes, because of the thunderbird within, as Stan Cuthand once explained.[20] The place was also a site for discussions between Crees and the British Crown.

After the initial meetings for Treaty 6 in 1876, *mistahi-maskwa* met David Laird at Sounding Lake in 1878. According to Laird, *mistahi-maskwa* said,

> as the Great Spirit had supplied the Indians with plenty of buffalo for food until the whiteman came, and as that means of support was about to fail them, the Government ought to take the place of the Great Spirit, and provide the Indians with the means of living in some other way.[21]

The term in Cree is *kâ-miyikowisiyahk*, "what the Creator has given us." Big Bear contrasts this with what the Queen is able to provide.

Another significant place in the landscape of the Cree is *mihkomin sâkahikan*. Peter Vandall, my great-grandfather, a direct descendant of *masaskêpiw* (the older brother of the influential Treaty 6 leader, *atâhkakohp*) and also the direct descendant of *wîhtikôhkan* (brother of the influential Treaty 8 leader *kinosêw/otay*), who raised him until he was fourteen, described the retreat of the buffalo into the ground as *kotâwîwak* ("they enter into the ground"). He also described the buffalo as "drowning themselves" (*ê-mistâpâwêhisocik*) in Redberry Lake (*mihkomin sâkahikan*). He did not see this happen, but he was raised by people who had. Redberry Lake was a place where people went to fast. They also talked about horses emerging from the water.

There are Cree origin stories in which the horses come from the water. The lake was also a place connected with "horse power." There are old stories in which people would bring their mares to breed by the lake. Spiritually powerful horses would emerge from the water to mate with the female horses. In some accounts, the horses are like people once they cross the edge of water back into the lake. Around the Battlefords area, for instance, some stories talk of the horses being like people once they pass through the surface of the water at *manitow sâkahikan*.

Places are important to the *nêhiyawak* and for identity formation. Clifford Sanderson, a respected storyteller and elder from the James Smith Reserve, spoke of *manitow sâkahikan* ("God's Lake" — Watrous, Saskatchewan, not to be confused with a lake of the same Cree name by Neilburg, Saskatchewan).[22] It is a sacred place where people would go to pray. People speak of its healing qualities. There is a stone there which fell from the sky. Grace Sanderson, Clifford's wife, said that people from all around could hear it when it fell from the sky, and came from all over to see it. It was a meteorite; it is flat with a square shape and lies at the bottom of the water. Clifford called it *sôhkêmakahk* ("it is powerful") to describe the power of the place (the stone in particular). The *nêhiyawak* go there to pray and leave tobacco offerings.

Charlie Burns from James Smith spoke about the significance of *manitow sâkahikan*:

> We used to go to Watrous and that lake, *manitow sâkahikan*, God's Lake, that's where we used to go and get that salt. We used to go and live there for two weeks. We would dry that salt and put it in bags. Then we would put it in a wagon and take it back to James Smith Reserve. People used to use that; that was a good medicine at one time.[23]

When asked what they used it for in particular, Burns responded, "Anything. You get cuts or any bruises, like eczema and all that. It was good. You wash your face with it."[24]

Communication with the Landscape and Other Beings

The locations noted were places where Cree and other Indigenous people communicated with the landscape. It is this communication that grounds Cree narrative memory. Through ceremonies, prayers, and songs, the *nêhiyawak* were able to communicate with other beings and the powers of the land around them, the *âtayôhkanak*, the spiritual grandfathers and grandmothers.

My great-great-great grandfather *wîhtikôhkân*, who died in 1914, was from the bush country around present-day Cold Lake, Alberta. He preferred to hunt with a bow and arrows. He had dream helpers, *pawâkanak*, who told him where game was. In our current reliance on technology, we have forgotten many things that this old man knew. My Uncle Burton Vandall told me that *wîhtikôhkân* could talk to animals. He would call out to them and they would come.

There is an interesting story regarding the power of the pipestem that has been passed on in my family. It is about the brother of *wîhtikôhkân*, *kinosêw* (*otay* in Dene, which means Jackfish). *kinosêw* entered into Treaty 8 in northern Alberta by taking the vow on his pipestem. His brother, *wîhtikôhkân* (my great-great-great grandfather), also had a pipe which could tap into the power of the land. ·

The pipestem is significant for the *nêhiyawak*, the Dene, and other Indigenous nations as a way of concluding arrangements. One could argue that it was a quintessential element of Indigenous religio-political protocol in large parts of Canada.

The pipestem was also more than merely a way of sealing political arrangements and treaties: rather, it was a way of making and affirming relationships with the land, of honouring the spiritual powers who dwelt where the people were living.

My father told me a story regarding the pipestem and *wîhtikôhkân*. Once when he was visiting my great-grandfather on a windy day, my great-grandfather told my father the following story:

> One time my grandfather [Peter Vandall/*kôkôcîs*] was in the house of *wîhtikôhkân*. It was an older house, and they were using a grease lamp for light. The wind crashed against the house and moved through the cracks of the house and the light of the grease lamp was almost extinguished. The house was rocking. . . .

My great-grandfather told my father that that was the only time he saw *wîhtikôhkân* scared:

> *wîhtikôhkân* was worried, because if he lost his house in the storm, he would be without shelter and in a difficult position. He took his pipestem, and pointed it in various directions and prayed to the various beings, including the wind spirit. He prayed that the wind would stop, and it did.[25]

wîhtikôhkân offered the smoke from the pipe to the wind and mediated the power of the spirit emanating from the wind. He was able to calm the winds by pulling out his pipe and praying.

The pipestem was also essential in the treaty-making process. One of the words associated with it is *asotamâkêwin*. The verb stem *asotamâkê* means "one makes a promise that cannot be broken." If one did break a promise, then that person would be affected by *pâstâhowin* — essentially, a deed that will come back to you: what you put in the world with one hand, you will eventually get back with the other. The consequences of the act will fall back on the person.

The stories of *mêmêkwêsiwak* also demonstrate Cree connection to the land. According to storytellers, the *mêmêkwêsiwak* are small beings, roughly two to three feet tall. They are usually found close to water, or in some cases pine trees. The pine functions as a gateway to the *mêmêkwêsiwak*, who come to people through dreams and direct them where to come. The dreaming person goes to that location, enters the realm of the *mêmêkwêsiw*, and presents cloth, tobacco, and hide as an offering. The *mêmêkwêsiw* then presents the dreamer with medicines. Stories from my reserve speak of *mêmêkwêsiwak* who have sand sculptures of human bodies in their water homes, which they use to make medicines.

In a 1976 interview, two elders from James Smith, Josie Whitehead and his wife, Helen, were asked if *mêmêkwêsiwak* ever died. They did not know

Grandmother and *wîhtikôhkân* (courtesy Grace Vandall).

the answer.[26] However, my Uncle Burton Vandall told me a story in which his grandfather, *pâcinîs* Vandall (Patrick Vandall), once found what appears to have been the body of a *mêmêkwêsiw* when he was surveying in northern Saskatchewan. He brought the *mêmêkwêsiw* back to camp, whereupon an old man told him to return the body to where he had found it. The experience left a deep impression upon him, and he talked about it for the rest of his life.

When the forces of colonialism exerted their full weight, people talked about the *mêmêkwêsiwak* retreating from the area in the same way the buffalo and the *âtayôhkanak* retreated. In the Qu'Appelle River Valley, people speak of how, after the flooding of the valley in the 1940s, the *mêmêkwêsiwak* who had played their water drums could no longer be heard. Similarly, Robert Brightman documents the retreat of *mêmêkwêsiwak* in areas of northern Manitoba.[27]

Cree narrative discourse not only involves human beings, but other beings such as *kihci-manitow/mâmawi-ôhtâwîmâw* (God), *âtayôhkonak* (spirit beings), and *kimosômipaninawak* (our grandfathers). This is a key component of the Indigenous way of seeing the world.

Dreaming the World

A dream helper, *pawâkan*, links a person to the rest of creation. A *pawâkan* could be any being, from a mosquito to a bear, and it imparts to its human counterpart various powers and abilities. In return for these gifts, the person treats the animal with respect and honours it. If the person has a bear for a dream helper, for instance, there may be dietary restrictions placed on eating bear meat. There may be songs that the person sings to his *pawâkan* that honour this being.

Clifford Sanderson told me that his grandfather, *asiniy-kâpaw*, had a bear as his dream helper.[28] The bear figures prominently in the worldview and belief system of Algonquian-speaking people. When *asiniy-kâpaw* died, a small bear came out of his chest and walked around. The bear, like the hummingbird (*âmow-piyêsîs*), was a source of medicine and healing. One reason is that these animals consume plants which themselves are medicines. Sanderson also told me a story about how, when one of his grandchildren was sick, he used a bear hide to help him: the baby lay on the hide for weeks and eventually got better.

The story of Andrew Ahenakew, an Anglican priest from Sandy Lake Reserve, and his acquisition of medicine[29] is a telling example. He had a dream about a bear who gave him medicine. The bear helper said:

I have come to give you my body, for since God made the earth, when
He made the animals, we are still as God had made us in the very beginning, we have no sickness in our bodies . . . Thus He has sent me hither
that I may give you my body for you to use, for you to make medicine
there from my body and to doctor people who are sick.[30]

Such stories demonstrate the importance of other beings to the narrative
memory of Cree people.

The *pawâkan,* one of the central features of Indigenous consciousness, allows people to tap into the land around them. "The *pawâkan,*" Brightman
writes, "is understood to assist its human dependent by providing 'power'."[31]
He notes the important Cree word *mamâhtâwisiwin,* which he translates as
"someone uses power."[32] Willie Ermine adds that "tapping into the mystery"
is a central process of Cree consciousness and knowing.[33] A person who is especially gifted in tapping into this power is called *omitêw.* Clifford Sanderson
used this term to refer to his grandfather, *asiniy-kâpaw.*[34]

Sarah Whitecalf also notes the importance of dream helpers in Cree
culture:

It is true that they used to look like human beings to the people, coming to tell them things, that is what is meant when one says, "she has a
dream spirit," that it looks like a human being to them, coming to teach
things, but in their sleep; and it is true that when they would try it, they
would indeed be able to do that which they had been taught.[35]

Ermine's concept of *mamâhtâwisiwin* as tapping into the mystery [36] is important in articulating a Cree concept of land. It also denotes how the *nêhiyawak*
can tap into the powers around them. It denotes, fundamentally, a way of
understanding things, of articulating a place in the world.

People use the images of technology to describe how Indigenous people
dwell in the world. The painter Norval Morrisseau, for instance, uses the image
of a computer as a metaphor for spiritual power.[37] He describes the centre of
spiritual power as the House of Invention, and uses the computer image to
describe this place. In contemporary Cree, the term *mamâhtâwi-âpacihcikan* is
used to describe a computer: it means, literally, "the machine which taps into
the mystery of life."

Morrisseau adds to the discussion of the importance of dreams through
his concept of the House of Invention,[38] which stands outside time and space

and is accessible through art and dreams. They don't represent any story at
all, Morriseau says of his paintings. They remind the viewer of the same experience that these Indian people, our ancestors, had in the dream world.
Reminding the viewer that he, too, can go there in his dream state.[39]

Brightman cites Michel Dumas, a Cree from northern Manitoba, who
describes a similar power that comes from the land of dreaming:

> People used to sleep in the water. You wouldn't believe it. They make
> a coffin. In the wintertime, they put them . . . like first freeze-up early
> bogs. . . . About March, about this time of year, they go and take this
> guy out. They stay there in the water and winter . . . he's dreaming at
> the bottom of the water. He's dreaming all the animals, they gotta come
> to him.[40]

The House of Invention can never be completely described, nor can one
person exhaust its possibilities. As Morrisseau says, "my grandfather told me
once that nobody, no matter how hard they tried, could remember all of the
legends; otherwise the whole of northwestern Ontario would be covered in
pictographs."[41] Thus, the artist, like the storyteller, is a participant in the per-
petuation of collective memory.

In the old days, people knew how to listen to the world; they relied on
dreams and intuition for knowledge through spiritual beliefs and practices.
nêhiyâwiwin, Cree-ness, involves thanking the Creator for the gift of life. Part
of Cree narrative memory involves the affirmation that there is a tie to other
beings. *kôkôcîs* said:

> *êkwa kîkisêpâ kâ-waniskâcik, nikî-pêhtawâwak mâna kêhtê-ayak;*
> *tâpiskôc ôma piyêsîsak kâ-kitocik kîkisêpâ k-âti-sâkâstêk ôma mistahi*
> *kâ-takahkihtâkosicik, êkosi anima kêhtê-ayak misiwê ê-kî-pêhtâkosicik*
> *ê-nikamocik – ahpô owîkimâkaniwâwa ê-naskwahamawâcik – iyikohk*
> *ê-kî-miywêyimocik aniki, mîna mistahi ê-kî-miywâsiniyik ita*
> *ê-kî-pimâcihocik.*

> And in the morning, when they arose, I used to hear the elders, just as
> the singing of the birds sounds beautiful in the morning, at day-break,
> so it was with the elders who could be heard all over as they sang — they
> would even sing in response to their wives — they took such pride in
> themselves, and their journey through life was very beautiful.[42]

Eli Bear echoes this:

> And I used to wonder when at the break of day he used to stand outside
> and chant, and singing to the sun. He used to do this using the four
> different directions and put words in the song. While he was doing this,
> I used to wonder why he did this for . . . but now I see what he was
> getting at.[43]

Through prayer and songs, the old people maintained ties to eternity and the
ancient memory of places.

In order to understand Cree narrative memory, one must understand Cree
philosophy and perspectives, *nêhiyawi-itâpisiniwin*. By understanding such
beings as the *mêmêkwêsiwak,* the *pawâkanak,* and the *âtayôhkanak,* one can
better understand the meaning of the collective experience of the *nêhiyawak*.
Mainstream historians often ignore such beings, or put them in the realm of
mythology, which removes a vital component from Cree narrative memory.

nêhiyawi-itâpisiniwin grounds stories within a framework and imbues
them with meaning. One cannot understand the Cree experiences of making
the transition to farming, engaging in treaty, and resistance to colonialism
without taking these elements into account. Such elements breathe life into
narratives and allow one to see life through the eyes of the *nêhiyawak*.

CHAPTER THREE

RETHINKING TREATY 6 IN THE SPIRIT OF *mistahi-maskwa* (BIG BEAR)

CREE NARRATIVE MEMORY starts with the living memory of our elders and storytellers, and their stories of connections to various places and events in the landscape. In this manner, the Cree treaty narratives become the basis from which the *nêhiyawak* can argue for their rights and place in Canada. They are also a way of understanding our collective worldview, epistemology, and our place in the world.

nimosôm (my grandfather, John R. McLeod) immersed himself in the sources of our collective memory by sitting with many elders in the 1970s. He was asked to organize the Treaty 6 Centennial Commemorations in 1976. He said:

> It was almost 100 years ago that our great grandfathers gathered at Fort Carlton and Fort Pitt to meet with Commissioners of the Crown in order to negotiate Treaty Number Six. Because of the importance of this and other treaties to Indian people, both in the past and now in the present, we shall be paying honour to our forefathers and the treaty which they negotiated for us and for our grandchildren.[1]

My grandfather knew that it was the treaty that was the foundation of our survival as Indians. He added:

Our elders tell us that the reason our people and our leaders went to Fort Carlton was to work for the survival of Indian people. One hundred years ago, they called upon the Queen to send her representations. One hundred years ago, they met with the commissioners and negotiated a treaty which allowed the Indian people to survive as Indians, and which allowed us to be here as Indians today and whatever the federal government or anyone else may say, without the efforts of our forefathers at Fort Carlton and Fort Pitt, we would not exist as Indians today.[2]

When I was younger, I used to travel with my grandfather to various gatherings. This time inspired me profoundly and left deep impressions upon me, and it is from these memories that I have been inspired to pursue my studies on Treaty 6.

mistahi-maskwa (Big Bear) is one of the most important political figures of the time to draw upon in a reassessment of Treaty 6. He was among the most respected leaders of the Cree and a strong resister of the British attempt to subordinate them. Sharon Venne describes the respect that *mistahi-maskwa* has in Cree culture:

Diamond Jubilee of Treaty 6, 1936 (Saskatchewan Archives Board, RA-1632-2).

Once I went with an Elder to the area known as Sounding Lake, which is in the eastern part of present-day Alberta. The Elder spoke about Big Bear and his ability to lead the people. During one huge gathering of over a thousand, Big Bear was the main Chief of the camp and all of the other Chiefs deferred to him. There was a dispute over a horse, which could have led to violence in the camp, but Big Bear rode among the fighting men and spoke to them. They stopped fighting at the request of Big Bear. He was a kind and fair man, which is the reason he receives such respect from the Cree People to this day.[3]

The territory of Treaty 6 covers much of central Saskatchewan and Alberta, which, until the 1870s, was heavily populated by buffalo, the animal that played a central role in the lives of the Cree.

The process of Treaty 6 formally began on August 18, 1876, when many Crees known as the House People and River People gathered at Fort Carlton (*pêhonânihk*). After holding a council, many House People entered into treaty with the British. On September 7, the treaty process continued at Fort Pitt (*wâskahikanis*) with many of the River People, some of the Beaver Hills People, and some Dene from the surrounding area.

The reason *pêhonânihk* and *wâskahikanis* were selected as sites of treaty negotiation was owing to their importance as gathering locations. The trading posts have been named *kihc-âtâwêwikamikwa* — literally, the "great houses of trade" — which denotes the function of these posts during the fur trade. Prior to the numbered treaties, there had been a period of roughly 200 years of mutually beneficial trade. The treaty process was in many ways an extension of the positive relationships that had emerged during this time. The notion of reciprocity (*miyo-wîcihitowin*, "helping each other in a good way") was the core of this relationship.

The Treaty 6 process continued. In addition to the people who took treaty after these initial meetings, many of the River People, including Lucky Man, Little Pine, and Thunderchild, entered into Treaty 6 by adhesion in 1879 at Sounding Lake. *mistahi-maskwa* himself did not enter into treaty until 1882 at Fort Walsh. One band — the Saulteaux of the North Battleford area — did not enter into Treaty 6 until 1956.

Treaty 6 was one of the numbered treaties that was negotiated throughout Canada, beginning in 1871 with the Saulteaux and Cree. The impetus for the negotiation of the treaties was the need for land for European settlers. There were friendship treaties with the Mi'kmaq and other nations in the east that predated the numbered treaties by at least 100 years, and later there were the Robinson Treaties of 1850. But the numbered treaties contain more explicit promises made by the Crown than previous treaties.

Another fundamental characteristic of the numbered treaties, particularly in the Treaty 6 area, was that the Cree were in some cases able to resist the Crown by force. Out of frustration and hunger, some men in *mistahi-maskwa*'s camp eventually took up arms, and only after the Northwest Resistance of 1885, *ê-mâyahkamikahk* ("where it went wrong"), did the Dominion of Canada begin to deal with the Indigenous people's opposition to expansion.

At their best, treaties represent the possibility of peaceful cohabitation and sharing of resources by two peoples. If this is to occur, of course, the Cree understanding of the treaty process must be taken into account. It is impossible to have genuine respect for people, and for different ways of seeing the world, without taking important cultural differences into account. In the case of the Cree understanding of Treaty 6, it is imperative to take into account the signers' oral understanding of the treaty. For a long time, mainstream culture has controlled the discourse between Euro-Canadians and Indigenous people; as a result, Treaty 6 has been understood primarily as a written document and the perspective of Cree people has been downplayed.

Cree camp at the elbow of the South Saskatchewan River
(Glenbow Archives, NA-1408-14).

Part of the treaty addresses not only a sharing of the resources of the land, but a sharing of understanding. This mutual understanding involves the intersection of both the oral and the written aspects of the treaty.

Many Cree elders have pointed out the inequities in how the treaties have been understood. They have also noted various levels of skepticism as to what transpired, and also about the written word. In 1975, during preparations for the 1976 centennial commemoration, Julian Moses commented about the written records of the treaty process:

> There is much written material but it was all done by non-Indians. When reading about the various treaties, all we see from the Indians are X's which may or may not belong to the same person, or even to Indians. Possibly the Indian people who were present at the signings had never held a pen before and did not know how to use one. We have never seen proof that the Indians did sign Treaties.[4]

Moses was correct in that only two headmen signed the treaty with their own hand: one signed in syllabics; the other, my grandfather Bernard Constant, signed using the English alphabet[5]; others simply touched the pen of the clerk, who then made X's on their behalf.

The Historical Context of Treaty 6

Treaty 6 must be understood in historical context as the product of a trading relationship that had existed between the Cree and the British, and later the Dominion of Canada, from 1670 to the 1870s. During this period, the Cree benefited greatly from commercial interaction with the newcomers and grew in both territory and prestige. For much of this time they functioned as middlemen, trading goods acquired from the British with other Indigenous groups. By the time of the treaties, the Cree had had a long-established relationship with the British.

The history of the interaction among the Cree, the British Crown, and later the Canadian government is grounded in early documents and political interactions. In contrast to the American policy of conquest, the British had a long tradition of negotiating with Indian people with regard to both economic and political activity. The foundation of the treaty-making process in North America was the Royal Proclamation of 1763, which mandated the Crown's responsibility to negotiate with Indigenous peoples as their lands were encroached upon. This important document also affirmed Indigenous ownership of traditional territories.

Treaty 6 occurred at a time of great change in what is today western Canada. The fur trade was on the decline, and the relationship between traders and Indians was consequently changing. As historian J. E. Foster writes, "Beginning in the 1840s and gathering momentum as the years passed were developments that spelled an end to the relationship existing between Indian and trader."[6] During this period, profits decreased and traditional fur trade activities shifted. John Milloy notes that, "In the period between 1850 and 1870 . . . the depletion of the buffalo herds brought the interests of the Cree and the traders into direct opposition, and a new phase of Cree-European relations, marked by hostility," began.[7] This is perhaps most evident in the process of Treaty 4, made south of Treaty 6, in which chiefs such as *kâ-kisîwêw* (Loud Voice), the Gambler, and *paskwâ* (Pasqua) all questioned the transfer of land from the Hudson's Bay Company to the Dominion of Canada.

Arthur J. Ray, J. R. Miller, and Frank Tough stress the importance of the fur trade in the long period of interaction between the Cree and the British: "The Cree and their allies had forged their relations with Whites within the context of the mercantile fur trade, which had been dominated by the HBC in its dual capacity as a trading company and representative of the Crown."[8] Foster describes the numbered treaties as opening up a new paradigm for the relations between the British and the Cree and other groups of the area; they signalled the end of the "compact."[9] He concludes that the British, instead of continuing a relationship of mutual benefit, became primarily concerned with land title. The Dominion of Canada's need for land for settlement, coupled with the decline of both the buffalo and the fur trade, brought about new landscape relations between the Cree and the British empire, of which Canada was a part.

John Leonard Taylor notes that the treaties, from the perspective of the people of Treaty 6, were a form of compensation for a new structure of land use — namely, agriculture.[10] The oral history of the Treaty 6 elders bears out this interpretation.[11]

Christianity was also part of this shift in lifestyle and ideology. The missionary John McDougall, the son of George McDougall, also a missionary, grew up speaking both Cree and Ojibway and was certainly familiar with the ways of western Indigenous people. He played a key role in the councils, and was initially welcomed by chiefs *mistawâsis* (Big Child) and *kâ-miyêstawêsit* (Beardy), who lived near Fort Carlton (*pêhonânihk*). However, he met firm opposition to the treaty process in the Fort Pitt area, which was occupied by the River People — perhaps because of his father's role in removing a *mistasiniy* stone from the Red Deer River in 1866.

The younger McDougall appealled to the Cree of the Saskatchewan River area, known as the River People, to take up farming. It is interesting to note that farming and Christianity go hand in hand, and that both signal a radical shift of worldview. While McDougall's message appealed to some, such as *wîhkasko-kisêyin*, there were others who questioned these new beliefs and practices.

In one of the council meetings before Treaty 6 in 1875, John MacDougall met *mistahi-maskwa* without *wîhkasko-kisêyin*. In the absence of *wîhkasko-kisêyin* (Old Man Sweetgrass, or simply Sweetgrass), *mistahi-maskwa* was the strongest chief in the area. He stated his opinion of the treaty-making process: "We want none of the Queen's presents: When we set a fox trap we scatter pieces of meat all around but when the fox gets into the trap we knock him on the head. We want no baits. Let your chiefs come like men and talk to us."[12]

mistahi-maskwa questioned the treaty process. McDougall tried to discredit *mistahi-maskwa* by calling him an outsider with no authority to speak for the people of the area. Alexander Morris, in his 1880 account, also attempts to discredit *mistahi-maskwa* by noting that he had "formerly lived at Jack Fish and for years had been regarded as a troublesome fellow."[13] Morris did not understand the complexity of the ethnicity of the Plains Indians at the time of treaty signing, particularly the relationship between the *nêhiyawak* and Saulteaux, describing them as disjointed groups: "Big Bear and his party were a small minority in camp. The Crees said they would have driven them out of camp long ago, but were afraid of their medicines as they are noted conjurers."[14]

Historian Laura Peers discusses the ambiguity of the names "Cree" and "Saulteaux" in the case of *mistahi-maskwa*. While *mistahi-maskwa's* father was Black Powder, a Saulteaux from northwest Ontario who came west — he was painted by Paul Kane in 1848 at Fort Pitt — *mistahi-maskwa* seems to have identified himself as Cree.[15] In an 1885 speech,[16] *mistahi-maskwa* identified himself as chief of the *nêhiyawak*.

More research needs to be done into the historical relationship between the Cree and the Saulteaux, but it is true that a Saulteaux in a camp of Cree was by no means an outsider, as Morris suggested. In the case of *mistahi-maskwa*, the point is not that he was part Saulteaux, but that he led a group of people who had elements of both cultures. Such cultural layering was common in Saskatchewan as well as throughout the northern Great Lakes region.

mistahi-maskwa and *wîhkasko-kisêyin*: Different Approaches to Treaty

In the fall of 1876, a messenger was sent to *wîhkasko-kisêyin* to tell him of the treaty talks,[17] but *mistahi-maskwa* was not informed of them. *wîhkasko-kisêyin* said, "God was looking down on us that day, and opened a new world" to the Indians.[18] However, not all Cree people were ready to embrace European culture as a solution to the massive changes they were experiencing, and *mistahi-maskwa* was one of them.

On September 5, 1876, Lt. Governor Alexander Morris arrived at Fort Pitt to continue Treaty 6 discussions. The people gathered there included some Cree and Saulteaux known as the River People, as well as some nearby Dene. Unlike the Cree who signed treaty at Fort Carlton, many River People were not Christians. In the area around Fort Pitt, some chiefs such as *wîhkasko-kisêyin* had adopted Christianity, whereas others wanted to keep their traditional lifestyle, centred on the buffalo. Because of his position, *wîhkasko-kisêyin* lost many supporters, and his "influence over the River Cree was exceedingly limited."[19] Because Ray et al did not examine the oral history of the people in their study, *Bounty and Benevolence*,[20] they give undue weight to the influence the Christian church may have had on *wîhkasko-kisêyin*: "Moreover, chiefs like Sweet Grass, a convert to Christianity, were probably influenced by the presence and words of Roman Catholic and Methodist missionaries."[21]

Morris provides more details about *wîhkasko-kisêyin's* actions and words during the signing: "Placing one hand over my heart and the other hand over his own, he said: May the white man's blood never be spilt on this earth. . . . When I hold your hand and touch your heart, let us be one."[22]

mistahi-maskwa must have been profoundly disappointed in *wîhkasko-kisêyin*, his one-time fellow *okihcitâw*,[23] because the latter signed the treaty without waiting for him to come and speak. "I find it difficult to express myself," said Big Bear, "because some of the bands are not represented. I have come to speak for the different bands that are out on the plains. It is no small matter that we were to consult about. I expected the Chiefs here would wait until I arrived."[24] From *mistahi-maskwa's* words, it would seem that the treaty process was prearranged, with little possibility for substantive dialogue between the participants. From the outset, leaders who were struggling to preserve the old Cree way of life were marginalized and excluded from the process.

Alex Stick, whose father was present at the signing of the treaty at Fort Pitt, portrays *wîhkasko-kisêyin* thus: "He did the business on the sly, he didn't notify any of the old people,"[25] adding, "The old people had a lot to say there, but it was too late as Sweetgrass had already given his commitment."[26]

The subversion of *wîhkasko-kisêyin* was important because it lessened resistance to the new order. Stick recounts that the year before the signing of Treaty 6, *wîhkasko-kisêyin* seems to have been influenced by an exchange of funds between him and a representative of the Hudson Bay Company: "The Store manager had sent him to the east coast. . . . someone there gave him money in a big box, it was a large amount of money. He took some of that money and brought it home. The rest he left there with the priests for safe-keeping."[27]

The treaty process lacked the flexibility to accommodate the viewpoints and wishes of Indian people. The terms had been predetermined, and it was only due to the insistence of the chiefs that the medicine chest was included in Treaty 6. In 1876, the *nêhiyawak* did have some bargaining power, but as the starvation years set in, the Cree were progressively unable to resist the new order.

John L. Tobias emphasizes that the numbered treaty process was far from ideal: "In 1871 Canada had no plan on how to deal with the Indians and the negotiation of treaties was not at the initiative of the Canadian government, but at the insistence of the Ojibwa Indians of the Northwest Angle and the Saulteaux of the tiny province of Manitoba."[28] D. J. Hall claims that Tobias "goes too far,"[29] but his position is similar to Tobias's in that he stresses Indigenous agency. Far from being passive participants in the treaty process, Hall argues that "the Indian not only forced major changes in the government's plan, such as it was, but raised most of the issues that appeared in subsequent treaties."[30] Indeed, there was a great deal of communication among Indigenous groups regarding the treaty process in Canada, and the resistance of *mistahi-maskwa* to Treaty 6 had historical precedents in the earlier numbered treaties.

Not quite a year after the Treaty 6 negotiations, in a letter to the Minister of the Interior, David Mills, Morris speculated on the effects that the death of *wîhkasko-kisêyin* might have on negotiations, noting that his "probable successor will be The Bear."[31] Morris noted that *mistahi-maskwa* had promised to take treaty,[32] but he argued that the shift of power from *wîhkasko-kisêyin* to *mistahi-maskwa* would cause difficulties:

I fear . . . that the loss of the influence of Sweet Grass will render the task of obtaining the adhesion of the Plains who were not present at

Fort Pitt, much more difficult than it otherwise would have been, and will lead to their making new and exaggerated demands.[33]

Morris feared that *mistahi-maskwa* would advocate for better terms. As a result, there would be challenges for the government as other Cree leaders followed suit.

mistahi-maskwa represented that part of Cree society that wanted to maintain the old way of life by hunting buffalo and preserving traditional ceremonies. Cree elder Robert Smallboy speaks for many when he says:

> Our grandfathers were smart, concerned about our lands and treaties. Another thing, from long ago, people survived on the buffalo. From the hides of the buffalo he made clothing for himself, moccasins, blankets and the skins were used to make his tipi. For this it seems the white man went after the buffalo, they tried to exterminate them. Our buffalo, the white man said, that this is why we signed treaties. The white man stole the buffalo for his own use and tried to kill them all.[34]

As long as there were buffalo, there was hope for those who wanted to hold on to the traditional way of life. As the great herds declined, the Cree became increasingly aware that they were at a crossroads, and that they would have to adapt to changing circumstances. Some chiefs, such as *mistawâsis* and *atâhkakohp*, were acutely conscious of the changes they were facing, and were willing to make accommodations in order to survive. Others, such as *mistahi-maskwa* and *minahikosis* (Little Pine), were more inclined to follow the dwindling herds. As long as the buffalo existed, Indians would not have to take rations and settle on reserves, and they would retain a measure of power.

During the negotiations, the issue of livelihood figured prominently in the minds of the leaders as they contemplated their future and that of their descendants. According to oral tradition, the chiefs of Treaty 6 did not surrender the right to hunt. "Livelihood, things like wild game, fowl, fish that you use, will still be yours," notes J. B. Stanley.[35] The testimony of Cree elders bears this out: "The wild game was to remain ours for hunting, trapping and also the fish were to remain ours."[36] Morris Lewis notes, "We promise you will not lose everything. For example, hunting, trapping, you will not lose these."[37]

Many elders speak of how their ancestors were assured that their traditional lifestyle would be preserved. "They said we have the rights to do these things," Robert Smallboy confirms. "Hunting, fishing and trapping are yours. The old people say these aren't given away."[38]

The importance of animals for the survival of Indian people is stressed: "All the game would remain theirs to live on. That's what they lived on, all the wild game. The Indians didn't give these away, they used them for themselves."[39]

Treaty promises regarding hunting point to a desire by Indians to hold on to their traditional way of life. *mistahi-maskwa* was one of the strongest advocates of this position, and his idealism and spirit inspired many during this troubling time.

From the left, seated: *atâhkakohp,* Flying in a Circle, and *mistawâsis.*
Standing: Louis O'Soup, NWMP scout and interpreter Peter Hourie
(Saskatchewan Archives Board, R-B2837).

CHAPTER FOUR

kâ-miyikowisiyahk

WHAT THE POWERS HAVE GIVEN US

AFTER THE INITIAL TREATY DISCUSSIONS, the Canadian government was anxious to get as many Cree bands as possible to enter treaties through adhesion. While there were assurances that Indians could continue hunting, there was a growing awareness that the buffalo were in decline. The relationship between the buffalo and the *nêhiyawak* was commemorated with *mistasiniy*, the Grandfather Buffalo Stone which was located at the westernmost tip of the Qu'Appelle River.

On August 13 and 14, 1878, David Laird, Minister of the Interior, went to Sounding Lake (*nipiy kâ-pitihkwêk*) to distribute treaty payments as well as to try to encourage other Indians to enter treaty. "I sent a messenger to warn both the Treaty and non-Treaty Indians of the meeting," he writes, adding, "The messenger met Big Bear and notified him and his band to come to Sounding Lake."[1] In contrast to what had occurred at Fort Pitt two years earlier, Laird was apparently trying to get as many Indian leaders as possible to attend.

The meeting seems to have been well attended. Laird writes, "On our arrival at Sounding Lake on the 13th August we found some twelve hundred Indians assembled among who was Big Bear, but I learned that he had only brought two or three members of his band with him."[2] *mistahi-maskwa* seems to have adopted a strategy of keeping some of his people away from the treaty talks. He knew that, in their state of starvation, many of them would be vulnerable.

mistahi-maskwa tried to get better terms than agreeing to settle on a reserve. "At one time," Laird notes, "he wanted to know if the Indians found what was promised in the Treaty was not sufficient for them to live upon, whether they could get more."[3] As recorded by Laird, *mistahi-maskwa* frames his discussion within the metaphors and symbols of Cree discourse. As the Great Spirit had supplied plenty of buffalo before the white man came, he says, the government ought to take the Great Spirit's place and provide the people with some other means of living.[4]

There are two important ideas here. First, the concept of what "the Great Spirit had supplied" is *kâ-miyikowisiyahk* — "what the Powers, including the Great Spirit and all of the ancestral spirits, grandfathers and grandmothers, have supplied." Second, *mistahi-maskwa* saw the government as an alternative food source, as another way of providing for the Indian people as the buffalo failed.

Laird was not persuaded by *mistahi-maskwa's* request: "In regard to Big Bear's request I would advise to do nothing for one band within the limits of a Treaty that is not done for all."[5] *mistahi-maskwa* is portrayed again as representing only a small number of people, and therefore his requests are dismissed.

When Chief Thunderchild, who had been a headman with *mistahi-maskwa*, took treaty at Sounding Lake in 1879, he also wondered whether the government would be able to provide for him as *kâ-kî-miyikowisiyahk*. As Norman Sunchild observes:

> At the time of the Treaty signing, Thunderchild was with Big Bear for three years. Within three years, they tried to starve him to death. The Government would not give him rations. In the third winter, when people were starving to death, forced to the point of eating dogs, he decided to enter into Treaty. He had thought about the Treaty. He was asked if he was the Chief. He answered, yes. He asked the whiteman [Edgar Dewdney]: How are you going to take care of me, are you going to take care of me like the Creator? The whiteman answered that he would use his power in the lands to take care of the Indian people.[6]

Here is the account of Sounding Lake from Thunderchild's perspective, as recorded by Edward Ahenakew:

> Before I signed the Treaty, I came to talk with Dewdney at Sounding Lake. "Are you O-ke-mow [the Leader]?" I asked him. "Tell me yes or no."

I asked him three times over, and he answered me each time, "Yes. I am O-ke-mow."

Then I said, "If I understand your words, is it that you can do for me as God had done for me?"

And he answered, "No. There is no two-legged man can do so."

"Then why do you want to take that power away from God?"

And he said to me, "What I can do, I will do humbly. You will not starve under me. Before I took the work, I looked at this paper (the Treaty) and I saw that it was just. I show it now before God, believing that it is true. This is Victoria's word."

But I asked him, "What is five dollars a head for this mighty land?" And we talked all that day.

Then he called out to the camp, "Wait, ye people. If I were an Indian, I would have this man for Chief. If you make him your Chief, you can use him well, for he is wise and he is young. Answer me."

And all the camp answered, "He will be our Chief."[7]

In response to the Cree who asked him questions like this, Edgar Dewdney, the Crown's representative, said, "No human walking on two legs will ever be able to break what I am hereby promising you. I will never pay you for your land, I will forever make continuous payments to you for it."[8]

This narrative is important because it is entirely consistent with Cree oral tradition. It also demonstrates the concept of *tipahamâtowin* within treaty discourse as remembered by the Cree: the phrase *kâkikê ka-pimi-tipahamâtân* is translated as, "I will forever make continuous payments to you for it."[9]

During treaty discussions at Sounding Lake in 1879, an old man named Chipmunk questioned the Crown's motives. I have reconstructed this narrative by drawing on the testimony of a variety of elders. John Buffalo remarked that, "after the commissioner spoke and spelled out his promises, one old man in the crowd stood up and denied all that was said. He said that 'it couldn't be possible.' The commissioner would not be able to live up to his promises."[10]

Lazarus Roan provides more detail:

A very old man stood up and said . . . "I don't believe what you are saying, does the Queen feel her breasts are big enough to care for us all, there are many of us people." The government official, named Edgar Dewdney, thought the old man was insane and suggested that he be taken away from this. It was that the old man was talking nonsense.

The official replied to him immediately, that the Queen [would] be able to feed the people as a mother feeds her children: "Yes, she has large breasts, enough so there will never be a shortage." It is unknown and interesting as to how the old man would have responded to the officials.[11]

James Bull knew the old man's reply: "You are telling us all this, you will never be able to treat us the way we are treated by Manito [*kâ-miyikowisiyahk*]. Look at this land with its abundance of food for us, you'll never be able to match that, you will not be able to do this."[12]

The Chipmunk questioned whether the Queen could keep her promises. He also doubted whether the Queen could provide for the *nêhiyawak* as the *kâ-miyikowisiyahk* had.

Nonetheless, the Queen was still understood within the kinship terminology grounded in the notions of reciprocity developed during the history of interaction between the *nêhiyawak* and the British Empire. In the Chipmunk narrative, the Queen is seen as a provider, like a mother. It should be noted that the word *kihci-okimâskwêw* has many layers of meaning. For instance, *okimâw* could mean someone who has authority, and someone who has corresponding powers: it also means chief or leader. A superficial understanding of the term would extend it to refer to a female because of the prefix *kihci-*. However, there is an older understanding of the term which refers to an older woman who is rich with relatives. It is not be surprising that the Cree would have used this term to describe the leader of the British Empire; she was understood as a female relative, but also as a being existing within a kinship structure.

mistahi-maskwa's Resistance

During the discussions at *nipiy kâ-pitihkwêk* in 1879 and until 1882, there was a concerted effort by many Cree leaders to establish a homeland in the Cypress Hills area. Edgar Dewdney resisted this effort and suspended rations to the bands involved. Throughout this period, many left *mistahi-maskwa*'s band because of impending starvation. When *mistahi-maskwa* took treaty he had a following of only 247.[13] It should be noted that the pipestem was not used when *mistahi-maskwa* entered into treaty.

From 1882 to 1885, *mistahi-maskwa* developed a plan of action. He wanted a series of contiguous reserves in south-western Saskatchewan. The significance of the Cypress Hills area was that it still had some buffalo, and it had been a historical meeting point for Indigenous nations. *mistahi-maskwa* thought that if all the people were together they would be stronger. He tried to have the terms of the treaty honoured, but to have better terms as well.

After his adhesion to the treaty, and before 1885, *mistahi-maskwa* continued to try to organize the Indigenous people of the prairie and parklands, to the concern of government officials. In the summer, Indian agent John M. Rae noted in a letter to Dewdney that "Carlton Indians are so hard up that they sympathize with the movement and I think they should be treated more liberally without delay."[14] Rae monitored Big Bear's movements. In a telegram to the Indian Commissioner he noted that "Big Bear left for Duck Lake."[15] Rae then recommended that people in Prince Albert should be advised of *mistahi-maskwa*'s movement. *mistahi-maskwa* was also in close touch with *payipwât* from the south during this period.[16]

In the summer of 1884, there was a large gathering on the Poundmaker Reserve. A Thirst Dance was held, as well as a meeting of the leaders who were most opposed to the terms of the existing treaties. During this time, one member of Lucky Man's band assaulted farm instructor John Craig. In response, Lawrence Vankoughnet, Deputy Superintendent of Indian Affairs, wrote to Dewdney on July 24, 1884: "I have to inform you that discretionary power may be allowed the agent in respect to giving moderate supplies of rations to Big Bear's band."[17]

The restraint that *mistahi-maskwa* exercised among the young men was considerable. He urged them not to harm the North West Mounted Police who had entered the Thirst Dance lodge to apprehend the individual who had assaulted Craig. However, Vankoughnet said there had to be limits to the level of support given, otherwise what had occurred in the Cypress Hills in the late 1870s and early 1880s, when widespread hunger and unrest among the First Nations in the area led to the eventual abandonment of Fort Walsh by the North West Mounted Police, would recur. He warned that there had to be moderation or "we shall have a repetition of the Fort Walsh mismanagement." He also noted that there was the possibility that they might have a camp "of all the idle Indians." One difference between the Cypress Hills situation and that of the Battleford area was that, in the former, there were "working Indians," leading Vankoughnet to conclude that, "if the Department undertakes to feed a camp of idle Indians, it can not expect work from the other Indians."[18]

In the winter of 1884-5, *mistahi-maskwa*'s band was becoming desperate. They had been forcibly removed by the government to an area near Frog

Lake in what is today northeastern Alberta. There the band was isolated, but it nonetheless attracted followers who resisted the treaty. There were reports that band members were trying to adapt to the new circumstances. In a telegram from Rae to Dewdney on January 13, 1885, Rae states: "Big Bear's men at work. Everything satisfactory." Francis Dickens, the son of English novelist Charles Dickens, NWMP commander at Fort Pitt, echoes this report,[19] but Dewdney takes a more cautionary approach: "This does not necessarily mean that they have settled down on a reserve, still it is only by careful and judicious treatment of these Indians that any advancement can be made and they prevented from being a disturbing element in the west."[20]

Nonetheless, Vankoughnet, in a letter dated February 5, 1885, warns that *mistahi-maskwa* and *minahikosis* (Little Pine) would move around; he wants to consult Dewdney "as to the best means of dealing with such Indians as not to incite or stir up other Indians on the Saskatchewan or elsewhere in the territories to act in riotous disorderly or threatening manner." This depiction of *mistahi-maskwa* as an outsider and a threat was perpetuated. Vankoughnet adds that "an example should be made of Chiefs or Indians" who continue to be troublesome; however, he notes that "great care must be taken that an efficient force of Police should be present to enforce any arrest that may be made."[21]

On February 12, in response to a letter from Vankoughnet, Dewdney writes that "it has always been my opinion that an example should be made of some of the leading Indians who incite or stir up other Indians to act in a manner threatening the peace of the Territories. . . ." He speaks of Indians who have been a "source of disquietude"; thus, there was continuous subordination of the traditional political structures of the Cree within the Treaty 6 area. Dewndey adds that strong steps would "help rid of us our most troublesome characters."[22]

mistahi-maskwa had spent much time and effort trying to organize the prairie chiefs in an attempt to get treaties honoured and improved. He had held meetings throughout Treaty 6 territory and consulted widely with other leaders. His efforts were monitored by the government. While he enjoyed a great deal of respect from other bands, there were tensions within his own. One of his younger sons, *âyimisîs* (Imasees), "was angry that his father had been attending meetings with other old men instead of picking out his reserve."[23] John Pritchard, a Métis interpreter from the Frog Lake area, describes *âyimisîs* at Big Bear's trial as "bucking against his father" — "when the father said anything the son bucks against it."[24]

Younger men in *mistahi-maskwa*'s band were disconcerted by the way in which the chief's efforts had failed to bring about security for the band. Many wanted more done to secure their own reserve so that they could settle down and make a living. Also, after almost a decade of trying to force the Canadian government to change its policies, many were tired of waiting.

Unfortunately, in the spring of 1885, tensions at Frog Lake grew. *kâ-papâmahcahkwêw* (Wandering Spirit), leader of the *okihcitâwak*, had many difficulties with Indian sub-agent Thomas Quinn. There was also tension between band members and the farm instructor, John Delaney, who was "heartily disliked by the Indians."[25] The festering tension eventually turned violent, and ten white residents in the Frog Lake area were killed on April 2, 1885.

Contemporary telegrams, many of them inaccurate, reveal a certain panic on the part of the authorities. On April 8 a telegram was sent from Qu'Appelle stating that "J M Rae Indian Agent killed by Big Bear." This seemed to reinforce the notion of *mistahi-maskwa* as being largely responsible for the tragic events of 1885. On April 9, a further telegram stated: "Nothing Authentic about J M Rae being killed." At Battleford, it was believed that it was "the intention of the Indians to exterminate the Whites," and there was a stubborn myth that *mistahi-maskwa* and others were working with Louis Riel. Another telegram from April 11 written by the Minister of Militia and Defence, A. P. Caron, noted that he "greatly feared" a massacre of all whites from Fort Pitt westward. On May 25, 1885, Major General Middleton sent a telegram to the Honourable Adolphe Caron, noting that *pîhtokahânapiwiyin* (Poundmaker) "was on his way to join Riel when he heard the news. Big Bear is not I suppose the only important Chief in arms. . . ."[26] It is clear from these telegrams that the government believed that Riel and *mistahi-maskwa* were working together, and that they had similar political objectives. However, the two leaders had little in common, personally or politically, and during the trials of 1885, it was noted that *mistahi-maskwa* had lost control of his band, and that *âyimisîs* treated his father with "utter contempt."[27] *âyimisîs*, along with this friend *kâ-papâmahcahkwêw*, had effectively taken control of the band.

The events at Frog Lake in 1885 were not surprising: after people have been starved into near-submission, violence may seem the only answer. The events of 1885 allowed Canada to subordinate the *nêhiyawak*. *mistahi-maskwa* was adamant that he had attempted to prevent bloodshed. He said at his trial:

Your Lordship, I am Big Bear, Chief of the Crees. The North West was mine. It belongs to me and to my tribe. For many, many moons I ruled it well. It was when I was away last winter when the trouble started. The young men and the troublemakers were beyond my control when I returned. They would not listen to my council.[28]

But the events of 1885 were not merely the actions of angry young men; they should be seen in a larger context. It should not be surprising that the younger men became tired with *mistahi-maskwa's* attempt to strengthen the treaties. It had been nearly ten years since Treaty 6 had been negotiated. The band had wandered widely in Canada and into the United States, and they had experienced severe hunger as they tried to make the transition to farming.

John Pritchard played a key role in the events of 1885, sheltering and protecting some of the people who were taken prisoner by Wandering Spirit and the *okihcitâwak*. At Big Bear's trial he testified to the role *mistahi-maskwa* had played in averting bloodshed, and the role he himself played in terms of protecting people's lives. He discusses the events at Fort Pitt, after the events which had occurred at Frog Lake: "Yes, the police got away, and it was Big Bear that tried to get them away."[29]

James Kay Simpson, another man interviewed during the 1885 trial, cited the frustration and the lack of influence *mistahi-maskwa* experienced. "He said they have been trying to take my name from me. I have always tried to stop the young men, and they have done it this time and taken my name from me."[30] *mistahi-maskwa* expresses remorse and notes that he tried to restrain the young men. In the trial transcipts it is noted that Big Bear did not have control over the band when it was at Frog Lake.[31]

Several chiefs, including *mistawâsis*, *atâhkakohp*, William Twatt, and John Smith from the Prince Albert area petitioned for *mistahi-maskwa's* release:

We believe that "Big Bear" is the only Indian of those concerned in the rebellion remaining in prison and although we have no sympathy with the heinous crimes laid to his charge, we humbly submit that it would be very gratifying to the Cree nation if her Majesty's Government would extend to this criminal the clemency shown from time to time to the other prisoners, and grant him pardon for the unexpired term of his sentence.[32]

There are several interesting points about this letter. The chiefs are trying to distance themselves from the events of 1885; they also go out of their way to appear to be those "who proved by our actions during the late unfortunate rebellion in the Territories our loyalty to Her Majesty the Queen." The image of the Queen as mother and provider is reinforced in the letter, Victoria being referred to as "our Great Mother."[33]

The letter is also important because it shows that *mistahi-maskwa*'s attempts to negotiate a better treaty were effectively over. It is the chiefs who pledge loyalty to the Queen who are speaking for him. The letter symbolically marks the collapse of the traditionalist element within the Cree leadership.[34]

Despite *mistahi-maskwa*'s weakened state, Hayter Reed, the architect of the federal government's draconian Indian agricultural policy, writing for Dewdney, notes the influence the old Cree leader still held:

> I beg to inform you that I believe the Commissioner, who is now absent from Regina, does not entertain an opinion favourable to the release at the present time, of Big Bear, as it is considered that members of his band settling down quietly with other Bands, would become disturbed and disorganized, and would, no doubt, desire to leave their present locations in order to join him.[35]

mistahi-maskwa's power was limited because of his health. Reed wanted it known that, if *mistahi-maskwa* was released, it was at the behest of the loyal chiefs: "I beg to suggest that the release should be made prominently to appear as having been obtained through the exertions of his loyal Chiefs, since that might tend to give them more influence with 'Big Bear'."[36]

mistahi-maskwa was released, but fell ill on his way home. He died on January 17, 1888. Reed notes the event in a letter of January 26, but he did not know the cause of Big Bear's death.[37] By that time, the core of the Cree leadership who had resisted the new order was in jail, in exile, or had passed away.

The Spirit of *mistahi-maskwa*

Understanding Treaty 6 is important in order to examine the moral foundations of Canada, given that the recent Royal Commission on Aboriginal People suggests that "Treaty promises were part of the foundations of Canada and keeping those promises is a challenge to the honour and legitimacy of Canada."[38] The story and spirit of *mistahi-maskwa* reminds us of this foundation.

At his trial said, the great chief said, "I am in chains. Never did I put a chain on any man. In my body, I have a free spirit. When I cross the wide river to the Sand Hills, that free spirit will go with me."[39] But whereas *mistahi-maskwa* was eventually put in prison, the buffalo were almost completely annihilated, and the pain of the residential schools is still very much alive, the subordination of the Cree people has never been complete. It was through the resistance of people such as *mistahi-maskwa*, and through the narrative of the old man at *nipiy kâ-pitihkwêk*, that the full story of Treaty 6 and the moral foundations of Canada come to light. These issues need to be rethought.

Big Bear in prison after *ê-mâyahkamikahk*
(Glenbow Archives, NA-1270-1).

CHAPTER FIVE

Spatial and Spiritual Exile

The stories of *mistahi-maskwa* show us the importance of the *nêhiyawi-itâpisiniwin* and the connection of the *nêhiyawak* to specific places. We see how *mistahi-maskwa* valued the old way of life and was reluctant to enter into a new one. After 1885, however, the government imposed a series of policies that stripped the *nêhiyawak* of our roots and caused us to move toward a state of spatial and spiritual exile.

Dwelling in the Familiar

To "be home" means to dwell within the landscape of the familiar, of collective memories, which was the world *mistahi-maskwa* was struggling to protect; it stands in opposition to being in exile. "Being home" means to be a nation, to have access to land, to be able to raise your own children, and to have political control. It involves having a collective sense of dignity. A collective memory emerges from a specific location, spatially and temporally, and includes such things as relationship to the land, songs, ceremonies, language, and stories.

nicâpân Peter Vandall, my great-grandfather, used to tell stories of Big John (his uncle, the son of *wîhtikôhkân*) and the Northwest Resistance of 1885, among other things, as a way of bridging the eternity of the past and the forever of the future with the infinity of the moment. Within *nêhiyâwiwin*, people are constantly weaving their personal narratives and traditional narratives. My family's stories were about surviving and remembering. When you remember, you know your place in creation.

Exile

A dominated group loses some of its narratives, while a dominant group attempts to impose its own. To describe this dynamic, I use the term "colonizer" for the group that has power, and "colonized" for the dominated group. These terms are not absolute, nor are they static, as many Indigenous groups later dominated by Europeans were themselves colonizers in their own right. The *nêhiyawak*, for instance, displaced other groups, such as the Blackfoot and the Dene, in their territorial expansion of the late 17th to the first half of the 19th centuries.

While it is important to recognize that the *nêhiyawak* were once a colonizing power, it is also true that British control over Cree territory, especially after *ê-mâyahkamikahk* (1885), radically altered our ability to govern ourselves and to perpetuate our stories. The British attempted systematically to alienate us from our land — and, in turn, from our collective traditions.

The process of alienation occurred in two interrelated and concurrent ways. Our alienation from the land was accelerated once the fur trade began to wind down and the treaty process was initiated, a process that was accompanied by increased settlement. Alienation from our stories and languages was brought about by coercive government policies and legislation, including the *Indian Act, 1895* (s. 114), that outlawed our religious ceremonies, and other policies that made attendance at residential schools mandatory.

The removal of an Indigenous group from their land can be defined as spatial exile. The *nêhiyawak* were taken from our lands and confined to small areas, and thus alienated from spiritual sites and sacred places such as *mistasiniy* and *mihkomin sâkahikan*. Once we were removed from our land and put on reserves, there occurred some erosion of our ties to these places.

The alienation of a group from its stories can be defined as spiritual exile. This removal from the voices and echoes of the ancestors is an attempt to destroy collective narrative memory. Spatial and spiritual exile both emerge from a colonial presence.

The notion of "coming home" is both temporal and spatial. It involves the traditional homeland of the *nêhiyawak* and also the way in which people try to move beyond the alienation experienced through colonialism. It is a spatial process in that all the *nêhiyawak* occupy landscapes with which they come into contact as they move through territory they had been prevented from dwelling in. "Coming home" is also a temporal process in that, through time, new experiences are layered on top of older ones described in the collective narratives. While "coming home" is a return to Indigenous memories and narratives, "home" has been changed through new layers of experience and new ways of occupying the same space. However, this is experience grounded in older memories and older narratives, which serve as a map for people to find their way through life.

Spatial Exile

Exile involves the removal of people from their land. Politically, ideologically, and economically, Indigenous groups have often been overwhelmed by larger groups, usually nation states. One could call this the colonization of Indigenous Being (of Indigenous worldview and life-world). It is the imposition on an ancient people of a new, colonial order and a new way of making sense of the world. The effects of this spatial and spiritual exile are devastating, as the alienation exists both in our hearts (spiritual exile) and in our physical alienation from the land (spatial exile).

Exile and colonialism for the *nêhiyawak* began in the 1870s, when the British Crown extended its influence into western Canada through the treaty process. The British had entered into treaties with the Indigenous people early on in their occupation of eastern Canada; however, the numbered treaties in the west made between 1871 and 1876 were more substantial than the earlier friendship treaties concluded in the east. The numbered treaties in the west covered large parts of Ontario, Manitoba, Saskatchewan, and Alberta. Many *nêhiyawak*, along with members of other tribal groups, accepted treaty because they saw it as their best chance for survival. The Treaty 6 area, from which most of the stories in this book come, covers much of central Saskatchewan and Alberta. During the negotiation of Treaty 6, the buffalo were vanishing and food was becoming scarce. The treaty promised help for the *nêhiyawak* in the form of a transitional agricultural economy.

After the treaties, between 1878 and 1885, the *nêhiyawak* were starving. The buffalo, their life blood, was almost extinct. The Cree world was under siege, and the ability to perpetuate *nêhiyâwiwin* was greatly undermined. Treaties and the incursions of Europeans upon the *nêhiyawaskiy* (Cree territory) transformed the land.

New Order upon the Land

My great-grandfather, *kôkôcîs* (Peter Vandall), lived at the crossroads of great historical and social changes, and had the good fortune of being able to sit with people who had experienced the changes of the 1870s and 1880s first-hand. *kôkôcîs* spoke of how, during those times of upheaval, the buffalo used to move in their thousands to Redberry Lake, south of the Sandy Lake Reserve, when the ice was thin. They would inevitably fall through the ice and drown — my great-grandfather used the expression *ê-kî-mistâpâwêhisocik*, which could be translated as "they drowned themselves." This happened because the order of the land had been transformed: instead of being able to roam freely, the buffalo, like the Indigenous people, were increasingly confined to smaller and smaller areas. The whole order of the landscape was radically changing. The Cree words for reservation — *askîhkân* ("fake land") and *iskonikan* ("leftovers") — echo this process of alienation, exile, and confinement.

One word that I have heard used to describe this time of change is *pâstâhowin*, which can be translated as "transgression" or "when one does something wrong it comes back to him"; retribution would be another translation. The word referred to how the changes brought about by Europeans caused various animals and spirit beings to retreat into the earth.

Despite the efforts of the *nêhiyawak* to resist the colonial presence, the events of 1885 strengthened the colonial grip on Cree territory. Out of desperation, frustration with the government, and starvation, events culminated in armed conflicts between Indigenous people and Canadians at Frenchman's Butte, Cutknife Hill, and Batoche. Edward Ahenakew, a Cree clergyman and one-time political activist, spoke of the "scars [that] remain in our relationship with the white man."[1] After the troubles, the Canadians dominated the new region: they imposed the new colonial order and met with markedly decreased resistance. The Cree word for the events of 1885, *ê-mâyahkamikahk* ("where it went wrong"), represents the culmination of spatial exile.

Spiritual Exile and the Residential Schools

In *Voices of the Plains Cree*, Edward Ahenakew created the semi-autobiographical character of Old Man Kiyâm to describe the spiritual exile that had been imposed on him and his people. The events of his life weighed him down; his attempt to overcome exile and find his way home seemed to end in failure. He compares himself to the *nêhiyawak* who lived a life of freedom:

The one brings to its song something of the wide expanse of the sky, the voice of the wind, the sound of waters; the other's song can only be the song of captivity, of the bars that limit freedom, and that pain that is in the heart. So it is with my spirit, which may try to soar, but falls again to the dullness of common things. . . ."[2]

Old Man Kiyâm feels imprisoned by time and space after *ê-mâyahkamikahk*, which signalled the end of freedom for Indigenous people in western Canada.

Exile is both physical and spiritual; it is the move away from the familiar toward a new and alien space. This new space attempts to transform and mutate pre-existing narratives and social structures. It was not only those old people like Old Man Kiyâm who were imprisoned and forced into exile, but also those who went through the residential school system.

Spiritual exile was the internalization of being taken off the land. A central manifestation of this was the residential school system, which was established as a way of "educating" and assimilating Indigenous people. There were many such schools throughout western Canada, operated by various churches. Children were taken from their homes and communities. Instead of being taught by their old people, they were taught in an alien environment that attempted to strip them of their dignity. The process amounted to cultural genocide. Once put away, in both a spiritual and a spatial sense, many children never came "home." Instead, they spent their lives ensnared in alcoholism and other destructive behaviours.

Gordon's Residential School (Saskatchewan Archives Board, R-B11423).

In her poignant paper, "The Disempowerment of First North American Native Peoples and Empowerment through Their Writings," Jeanette C. Armstrong writes: "Our children, for generations, were seized from our communities and homes and placed in indoctrination camps until our language, our religions, our customs, our values and our society structures almost disappeared. This was the residential school experience."[3] The schools also severely disrupted the transmission of language and stories.

In the 1930s, *nimosôm* (my grandfather) went to a residential school on Gordon's Reserve, north of Regina. At first, he was happy to go; a friend of his, Edward Burns, even remembered him clapping his hands in anticipation.[4] He was anxious to see the world beyond the borders of the reserve. His experience of the school, however, was far from what he had expected. He escaped and came back to the reserve and told his father, Abel McLeod, what was going on there — beatings, children going naked and hungry. *nimosôm* remembered having pity on one young boy, who would cry because he was homesick, and *nimosôm* did his best to take care of him.[5]

The authorities came for *nimosôm* a second time, but *nicâpân* did not want his son to go back. The Mounted Police told him that they would arrest him if he resisted. The police knew that *nicâpân* was a man of influence, and that an arrest would be difficult because the community supported him. When he told the police, "Well, you will have to arrest me. I can't let you take my son again," they forcefully removed *nimosôm*, a boy of twelve, who spent the next three nights in successive jails as he was taken back to the school.

Children playing at a residential school, c. 1920s
(Saskatchewan Archives Board, R-DQ-A35).

He escaped again, but his experience exemplifies the process of spiritual exile. Alienation from the land, political pressure, and the use of force were all part of a larger effort to destroy *nêhiyâwiwin*. The government even amended the *Indian Act* in 1927, making it illegal for Indians to collect money to fight for the protection of their treaty rights. *nicâpân* was active in the political struggle, and in 1932, he went with John B. Tootoosis and five others to Ottawa to fight for Indigenous rights, despite the provisions of the *Act*.

The narrative of *nimosôm* maps onto an old prophecy told by Frizzly Bear, an elder from the *wîhcêkan sâkahikan* Reserve in north-central Saskatchewan. The prophecy dates from the late 19th century: "If you don't agree with him [the white man], he'll get up and point at you with a revolver, but he can't fire. He'll put his gun down and everything will be over. You will agree with him and what he's going to teach you is nothing that is any good for us."[6] Frizzly Bear tells also of a prophecy that representatives of the government would use force to take children from their homes and communities. Many of the survivors of these schools are modern-day *okihcitâwak*; instead of fighting in the physical world, they fight against the memories of the schools.

John Tootoosis says of the residential schools: "They washed away practically everything from our minds, all the things an Indian needed to help himself, to think the way a human person should in order to survive. . . . We were defenceless."[7]

Spatial exile occurred first, followed by spiritual exile. Frizzly Bear describes the spatial exile as prophesied by the Old People: "You won't be able to stop anywhere on your journeys because there will be a steel rope everywhere."[8] The rope would cut the land into sections, for it is "the wire they use for fencing."[9]

The prophecy that Frizzly Bear speaks of came true.

CHAPTER SIX

Coming Home through Stories

DESPITE THE ENCROACHING PRESENCE OF SETTLERS, the *nêhiyawak* continued to resist colonialism and exile, and many people retained the echoes of Cree narrative memory. Some of the strongest leaders of this resistance were *mistahi-maskwa*, *minahikosis*, and *payipwât*. There are many stories of resistance to the colonial order.

Playful and Humorous Treaty Stories

One of the ways in which the *nêhiyawak* and the Métis survived the onslaught of colonialism was through humour. My father told me how his grandfather, *kôkôcîs*, used to speak of old men at Batoche who told jokes to comfort themselves while they were being shot at. Without humour, the tragedy of spatial and spiritual exile would have been unbearable.

There is an anonymous resistance story about the treaties:

So I'm going to tell a story about this woman who was kind of spry. She knew five dollars [the treaty annuity] wasn't enough. So she got this notion to get herself pregnant as she'd get paid in advance. She put a pillow under her skirt; so she walked up the paymaster. When he saw her he said, "So you're pregnant. Then we'll have to pay you an extra five dollars in advance." When she received her money she fumbled a dollar bill on to the floor, then she bent down to pick it up. Her string bust, and she had a miscarriage; her pillow fell out. So this was the end of advances on pregnant women. They have to be born before they receive $5.00. This is the little story that I wanted to tell.[1]

The story relates an interesting encounter between the new colonial order and the *nêhiyawak*. Though while humorous, the story is about resisting the imposition of treaty and the reserve system. Forced to live on reserves, the *nêhiyawak* practised passive resistance. Such stories seek to transform the circumstances people were enduring.

My uncle Burton Vandall told me another humorous story:

At treaty payment time, people would borrow children from other families. They would walk up to the paymaster, who was handing out treaty annuity payments, over and over again; everyone would take turn using the same children. Eventually, the paymaster caught on, and he started to paint a mark on the faces of the children once they got their first and "final" payments.

The narrative makes fun of the situation in which the *nêhiyawak* found themselves. The story is a true account, but it satirizes the regulation of daily life among the *nêhiyawak*.

One of my ancestors, Big John Janvier, *kôkôcîs*'s uncle, adopted elements of the colonial presence and transformed them to subvert them. He was a successful farmer on the Sandy Lake Reserve and taught *kôkôcîs* how to farm. Big John was also a photographer, and took pictures of white farmers near his reserve. He had a darkroom in his basement. He also had a Bible in Cree syllabics, which he read regularly. But while he adopted a form of Christianity and elements of modern technology such as the camera, he was still a Cree.

Big John's father was *wîhtikôhkân*, a multilingual Cree/Dene from the Cold Lake area and the brother of *kinosêw*, an important Cree/Dene leader during the Treaty 8 negotiations. Because he played an important role in raising my great-grandfather, I was interested in how this old man influenced my great-grandfather.

When I asked my father how *wîhtikôhkân* conceptualized Christianity, he said, "They talked about Indian philosophy, which was very synonymous to Christianity. . . . the transition for him was not a big issue." My great-grandfather wove the narratives of Cree/Dene hunting beliefs into those of Christianity and found ways to apply old concepts to new situations. While *wîhtikôhkân* used dreams and intuition, Big John, his son, used some of these techniques only in the new context. "He really believed in God," my father noted. "Those old people who raised him talked to him about God."

There is an interesting story of how *wîhtikôhkân* would go into the church. The word he used was *kî-sâh-sîhcisiwak* ("they sat crowded together"):

> He was sitting in church and this man was preaching. He used to go there and smoke his pipe and listen. Mostly he went because the minister at the time used to invite him. He tried to solicit him to turn to Christianity. Out of the kindness of his heart, *wîhcikôs* [*wîhtikôhkân's* nickname] used to go to listen and smoke his pipe. He couldn't understand why they would talk about Jesus that they would save human beings yet they killed him. He used to think they were afraid that they killed him and that they would be punished. He used to think these people were afraid.

kôkôcîs was raised by an old hunter who, while curious about Christianity, saw the contradictions in it as well as how it was used to scare people.

Big John Janvier (courtesy Grace Vandall).

My great-grandfather went to day school on the reserve for two years. He laughed when he told about his experience there: "They didn't teach me anything. . . . all they had me do was write on a slate." His education came from the old man *wîhtikôhkân*, who took in his grandson at an early age (my great-grandfather's mother died when he was quite young). The old man raised him until he was fourteen, then Big John took charge and taught my grandfather about farming.

Unfortunately, Big John died during the influenza epidemic of 1918; but he represents the transition period when people were moving from hunting to farming. My father remarked, "At the time when people were forced to move on to the reserves, he adapted quite rapidly." My father shared the following narrative with me regarding Big John:

> He used to look at the soil and he could tell by its texture how fluffed up it was, the colour of it was grey-light, it was worked properly. It had to do with circulating the soil once a year. He used to plough his land about six inches deep . . . no deeper than that. He would do this every year so the soil kept circulating. He studied the texture to see how much fibre there was in it. It was almost like he could feel the land. . . .
>
> I always remember my grandfather telling that Big John was a very strict person in terms of discipline . . . even to break a handle of a fork was a very severe situation because at that time fork handles were not easy to come by and the handmade ones were not like the bought ones. Big John set him up with two oxen and he showed him everything he knew about farming.

kôkôcîs studied the techniques Big John used:

> My grandfather really liked farming. He liked working with animals and liked working with the land. He studied and kept a diary every year of his farming. Every year, he studied this diary to find ways to improve it. It was a science for him. He wrote everything in Cree syllabics . . . and it was in his heart to farm.

Even though people began to farm, they still hunted. My father noted: "They used to go hunting in the fall. He [my great-grandfather] used to go hunting for wild meat and we would live on it in the winter."[2] In my own childhood, when we lived in the city, wild meat was an important part of our diet.

These men had a profound effect on *kôkôcîs*. Historian Maureen Lux notes that 50,000 Canadians died from influenza in the epidemic: "During the epidemic the Royal Canadian Mounted Police (RCMP) were sent to reserves to enforce strict quarantines, preventing Native people from leaving reserves."[3] The sickness had a heavy impact on the people. This sickness, my father told me, caused Edward Ahenakew to want to be a doctor. He saw so many of his people suffer that he wanted to help them. Stan Cuthand confirms the story: "It was during these hard times with so many funerals that Edward Ahenakew decided to study medicine and become more useful to his people."[4]

Another thing that changed was how people took care of their health. Old Man Kiyâm, the semi-autobiographical voice of Edward Ahenakew, reflects on the changes affecting Crees: "Indian dances, they tell me, are a thing of the past, and they have adopted the white man's way of dancing instead. No conjurer visits the sick, but the white man's doctor is called to give his medicine to the ailing."[5] But this is not completely true. Some families on the Sandy Lake Reserve held onto traditional healing techniques well into my lifetime.

Vandall family photograph, c. 1910. Back row: *pâcinîs*, unknown, unknown, Big John, unknown, Fred Vandall, unknown, Gabriel Vandall.
Centre Row: *kôkôcîs*, unknown, unknown, unknown.
Front Row: unknown, unknown, unknown, *kwêcic*, *cîhcam* (Maria), Maria, Sarah Rabbitskin, baby Alex Vandall, unknown, baby unknown.

kôkôcîs's paternal aunt, *kwêcic*, for example, knew various plant remedies and helped the people when they were sick.

My father told me the following story, which *kôkôcîs* had told him. During 1918-19 an old man had a dream about a medicine he could use from skunks, which would help the people get better. This old man then told *pâcinîs's* second wife (*pâcinîs* was *kôkôcîs's* father, and the brother of *kwêcic*). This woman, Sarah Rabbitskin, was from the nearby reserve of Big River. The dream told the old man that the skunk would help them in this time of trouble, which proved to be quite useful. Many people were saved because of the knowledge that was given to the old man in his dream. My aunt, Barbara McLeod, who taught at the Big River Reserve decades later, said that there was still knowledge of this skunk medicine there.

Despite the shifts occurring in the people's lives, they still relied a great deal on older ways of doing things, including traditional medicinal practices. Members of my family have told me that people came from all over — some from as far away as Montana — to see *kwêcic* to get medicine for a variety of ailments. She died at the age of 110 when I was seven or eight.

There has been a shift from traditional healing techniques to modern ones, but one has to be careful in ascribing the cause. It was not simply the shift to Christianity and farming that brought about the change, for during that transition time people still relied on plants, animals, and dreams for treating ailments, and they worked quite effectively. Gradually, however, people began going to hospitals more often, and the old techniques fell out of use.

Exile

I would like to share one exile story about the troubled times of 1885. My great-grandfather, *kôkôcîs*, told this story at *nôhkom's* (my grandmother's) funeral. It is also recorded in *The Stories of the House People*.[6] *kôkôcîs* opens the story:

> *aya, ê-kî-âcimostawit ôtê ohci kihci-môhkomâninâhk — nitôtêminânak*
> *êkotê itâmowak ôta kâ-mâyahkamikahk — êkwa, êwako awa pêyak nisis*
> *aya, kî-pê-takohtêw tânitahtw-âskiy aspin ôma otâhk*

> It was told to me by a man from the United States — friends of ours had fled there at the time of *ê-mâyahkamikahk* — and this one was my uncle, he had come back a few years ago.[7]

Through the storytelling, the uncle comes home from exile; he has managed, through the humour of the stories, to preserve his dignity as a *nêhiyaw*. It is through these stories that the people attempted to find a way home. *kôkôcîs* spent the whole day with his uncle, listening to his stories. *kôkôcîs* reported that his uncle said, "I do not have much to give you, but I will give this story, my nephew."

The story is about a man who went fishing. This man liked to drink and was sipping whiskey while he was fishing. He needed bait and saw a snake with a frog in its mouth. The man took the frog out of the snake's mouth, but he had pity on the snake, for he knew that the snake was as hungry as he was. This man, after taking the frog, gave the snake some whiskey in exchange. After a while, the snake came back with another frog.[8]

This uncle of *kôkôcîs* had fled during the troubled times, forced into exile because he had made a stand for his rights and dignity. The story was given to *kôkôcîs* and was an important part of his repertoire. It speaks of being generous and of having pity on those with less power. It talks about the changes, and the effort on the part of people who were trying to negotiate this emerging space.

Coming Home through Stories

The effects of going to school have to be understood as a radical separation from the past, a disjunction in the daily experience of the people. They were no longer allowed to acquire language and socialization in the traditional way. Their economic life had also changed, and affected collective narratives. Twentieth-century *nêhiyawak* became increasingly aware of the limitations being placed upon them, and of the systematic attempts made to eradicate their culture. Being in exile, and the trauma associated with it, are manifested in the stories.

Our fight to survive as a people goes beyond the issue of residential schools. Smith Atimoyoo, one of the founders of the Saskatchewan Indian Cultural College in Saskatoon, spoke of the "new arrows" Indian people now have at their disposal to fight for our collective existence.[9] Words are like arrows that can be shot at the narratives of the colonial power.[10] Word-arrows have transformative power and can help Indigenous people come home. They help to establish a new discursive space. Every time a story is told, every time one word of an Indigenous language is spoken, we are resisting the destruction of our collective memory.

Through stories, we can find our place in the world. The character of Old Man Kiyâm struggles to find his place in the world through stories. Edward Ahenakew writes that, after failing in the white world, Old Man Kiyâm "reverted to the old Indian way of life, allowed his hair to grow long, and he chose to wander from house to house, reciting old legends, winning a reputation for himself as a storyteller."[11] He was trying to make sense of the present from the experiences of the past.

Stories act as the vehicles of cultural transmission by linking one generation to the next. There are many levels to the stories, and many functions to them: they link the past to the present and allow the possibility of cultural transmission, and of coming home in an ideological sense. Our contemporary task is to retrieve tribal narratives and paradigms and to reaffirm our identities in the face of the overwhelming pressure of exile and colonialism.

"Coming home through stories" happens in everyday life. One day I was in a small-town café with my father and Edwin Tootoosis, near my reserve. My dad and Edwin told old stories in Cree for about two hours. Everyone kept staring at us, as though we didn't belong, as if we had no right to be there. But Dad and Edwin kept telling their stories; they chose to retain their dignity through the language and the stories instead of passively letting someone control them. When we walked out of the café, everyone, in their silent way, acknowledged what had happened. The feeling was familiar: the phrase "damned Indians" had been heard all too often. That day, the hope of spring, the breaking of the ice, filled the air; the rebirth of possibilities, of the turning of eternity, penetrated the space around us, creating calmness.

As we walked toward our trucks in the street, my dad told another story:

A long time ago, an old man and his grandson went to town. The boy was about fourteen. They had gone to town to buy groceries. They milled about the store and collected the items that they needed. After they had filled their cart, there was a man by the door. He said to his friend, "Damn lazy Indians." The man then went up to the old man and said, "You are god-damn lazy. Why can't you just stay on the reserve, where you belong?" The taunts continued, but the old man kept calm. After they gathered their groceries, they stood outside their vehicles. The grandson asked, "*nimosôm*, why didn't you say something to that man who was there, who was saying those things to us?" The grandfather answered his grandson with another question:

"How long were we in the store?"

"Well, we were there for five minutes."

"Yes, my grandson. We were in that store for five minutes. We had to deal with that man for five minutes. But he has to deal with himself for the rest of his life."

As I understand this story, the way to survive is not by giving in to hatred, but by concentrating on positive things, like retrieving stories. This is a form of passive resistance, in the spirit of Gandhi. On reflection, I am pretty sure that it was my father and my grandfather who were the characters in the story.

I will tell one more story. In 1976, *nimosôm* was chosen to be the organizer of the Treaty 6 centennial commemorations. He travelled around the province and listened to old people, sometimes taking me along. At the time of the commemorations at Onion Lake, *nimosôm* translated for Jim Kâ-Nîpitêhtêw:

He says, "There was this body that needed someone." And he says, "And I guess that this was the one that was placed in this body." He says, "I hope when I leave this body, I will leave it beautiful." And he says, "When you see that spruce, when it is just born, and that spruce, as it grows, is beautiful. When the spruce stands up and meets you, it meets you with dignity because he has lived his life the way he was placed here." He says, "Everyone of us is beautiful. We should leave our bodies with dignity."[12]

I think what *nimosôm* was saying, as he translated from Jim Kâ-Nîpitêhtêw, was that a human being is like a tree. Like all organisms, it grows and matures over time. The tree has a certain nature which, if nurtured, allows it to grow. If a person lives a life grounded in his own stories and experiences, he will be able to live in dignity and greet the day and all the things that happen to him. The process of living, of which I still know very little, is an accumulation of years of experience and growing. However, stories, as such people as Jim Kâ-Nîpitêhtêw, *nimosôm*, John Tootoosis, Keith Basso,[13] and Julie Cruikshank[14] have said, ground a person. Stories act as foundations on which we can live our lives.

I think of *nêhiyâwiwin*, or Cree-ness, as a large, collective body. When I was born in 1970, many people knew many beautiful things about *nêhiyâwiwin*. As *nêhiyawak*, when we listen and tell our stories, when we listen and hear our language, we have dignity because we are living our lives as we should, on our own terms. Our stories give us voice, hope, and a place in the world. To tell stories is to remember. We owe it to those still unborn to remember, so that they will have a home in the face of diaspora.

In a sense, "coming home" is an exercise in physical and spiritual cartography. It is trying to locate the place of understanding and culture. It is the attempt to link two disparate narrative locations, and to find a place of speaking wherein the experiences of the present can be understood as a function of the past. At the same time, culture is a living organism, with many layers and levels, and there will always be manifold interpretations. I would argue, as David Newhouse dooes, that emerging forms of Aboriginal consciousness, including Cree ones, will be hybridized.[15]

To come home through stories is to anchor ourselves in the world. Many people tried to make sense of their experiences. They survived the residential schools and attempted to make sense of the world around them. While being thrown out of their spiritual home, they were able, through tremendous effort, to find their anchor again and to come home through stories and narrative memory. Thanks to them we have that anchor today. It is now our time and our responsibility to keep the anchor, if Cree narrative memory is to survive.

CHAPTER SEVEN

pîkahin okosisa

A Cree Story of Change

COMING HOME THROUGH STORIES involves the attempt to recover collective narrative memory and to reconnect to the territory of our ancestors. Part of this process of connecting to land and the experiences of Cree people is to see the world through Cree eyes. One of the central ways of doing this is to engage the *âtayôhkêwina*, the sacred stories, and to undertake an exploration of spiritual history. The story of *pîkahin okosisa* is a prime example of this.

The story of *pîkahin okosisa* took place on my reserve, *nihtâwikihcikanisihk* (the James Smith Reserve), in north-eastern Saskatchewan. My great-great-great grandmother, *kêhkêhk-iskwêw* (Betsy McLeod), was present when it occurred. She told the story to my late *mosôm*, John R. McLeod, who, in turn, told it to my father, Jerry McLeod, who, in turn, told it to me. My understanding of the story was also nourished by other storytellers: Bill Stonestand, grandson of *asiniy-kâpaw;* Charlie Burns, great-grandson of *iskôtêw;* and Clifford Sanderson, also a relative of *asiniy-kâpaw,* a ceremonial leader on the James Smith Reserve.

The process through which I learned the story is an example of "coming home through stories." It allowed me to connect to a time that stretched far before my birth. By learning the stories that formed my grandparents and made them the people they were, I developed deep and long-lasting ties with various people. As I often tell my students, the way in which we do oral history is more important than what we find out. Learning the story also gave me an excellent opportunity to develop my skills in the Cree language.

I have spent many years being fascinated by this story and gathering the details of it. I have written it down because it seems to be my reserve's core narrative that describes the massive changes of the early reserve period.

Another thing that was made clear to me when I was listening to this story is that oral traditions are dynamic and can have different meanings in the same community. Oral cultures are multi-layered, but so are written ones; there is constant play among different layers of understanding. These stories are embodied memory, and they profoundly influence how we live and understand our lives.

While the old people I visited shared a common story, and they all spoke Cree, they had various understanding of the significance of *pîkahin okosisa*. The storytellers layered ancient Cree memory in different ways; some had adopted Christianity to varying degrees. Hearing these various storytellers, I was able to see different nuances of the story.

Historical Context of the Story

The story takes place during a time of great change for the people of my band. They were making the transition to reserve life and experiencing firsthand the limitations of the new *Indian Act*. Many people were making the transition to Christianity as well. There was a story of someone from the nearby Red Earth Reserve who was to get a name. The Reverend Hines, a well-known missionary in western Canada, suggested that the Cree take his name, but the Cree from Red Earth said, "No, I would rather have the name Jesus."[1]

The story of *pîkahin okosisa* takes place in the same year that *manitowêw* (Almighty Voice) died in a violent confrontation with the Mounted Police. The story of *manitowêw* adds another dimension to what Cree people were experiencing during this period. *manitowêw*, a recently married man from the One Arrow Reserve, had killed a cow in order to feed his family. Charlie Burns says that the farm instructor told him, "you've done a bad thing to kill a cow. You shouldn't kill that cow. That old man told him that my kids got nothing to eat." Burns added, "They went and got him and they put him in jail at Duck Lake." However, he was not kept long: "They kept him there . . . for two nights I think, the third night he ran away . . . he bust a window."[2]

manitowêw fled to the nearby One Arrow Reserve: "They dug a hole there and then that's where he used to hide. And . . . his grandmother . . . had a bed right in the corner. And what they done they put sticks over that, and that old lady uses it there. Until the police are gone."[3] *nicâpân* also told me this story.[4]

Finally, *manitowêw* went on the run. The police chased him for two years. A scout from James Smith, Sam Smith (a nephew of James Smith), who was known as Sam Police, led the trail to *manitowêw*: "In a little hill. I guess he dug a hole there. And the policeman knew that he was there. And he hollered at Sam Police, '*tapasî!* Run away. I want to kill all of your Mounties — your friends'."[5]

Fighting started and *manitowêw* "killed eight policeman."[6] But *manitowêw* died as well. It is said that, as he died, he sang his death song.

The story illustrates how the new system of life was exceptionally hard on Indian people: a man who was trying to provide for his family was chased for two years because he killed a cow. The story also shows the power that the new order had over Indian people.

pîkahin okosisa: The Story

The story of *pîkahin okosisa* is situated around a group of people from the *cikâstêpêsin* (Shadow on the Water) Reserve south of Prince Albert. The reserve was named after the first chief, *cikâstêpêsin*. His brother-in-law (they were married to sisters) was *pîkahin okosisa*, who, in turn, was closely related to Big Head, a headman of *cikâstêpêsin*'s band. Both these names were derived from water, but neither man was baptized, as Clifford Sanderson points out.[7]

My father told me this story:

There was a large flood on Sugar Island [*sôkâw-ministik*], which is close to Birch Hills, Saskatchewan. Many people died during this flood. There was one woman who climbed up a tree with her baby; she tied a cloth around the tree and moved up the tree to escape the water. The cloth was used to hold her up there. Eventually, the flood went away, and the people left the area. It so happens too that about eleven people from the band had been involved in the troubles at Batoche in 1885. There were too many bad feelings associated with the land there, at Sugar Island, so they left. Some of them went to camp with the people of the James Smith Reserve. However, a group also went to the Sturgeon Lake reserve.

The camps were close together, for the people shared with each other, and they took pity on their fellow *nêhiyawak*. Clifford Sanderson says that people camped near the SaskPower station close to Kinistino. That is why the people of *cikâstêpêsin* stayed there.

pîkahin is derived from a verb stem that means "to stir water." *pîkahin okosisa* died about 1897, twelve years after *ê-mâyahkamikahk*, the resistance of 1885. Charlie Burns said, "*ê-kî-âhkosit*" (he was sick).[8] My father said that, after *pîkahin okosisa* died, they wrapped him up in cloths, and an old woman was in charge of taking care of the body. While she was changing the wrappings, she noticed that his left side was warming up. Then the man came back to life. He rose on the third day, "like God,"[9] "and he got up."[10] Charlie Burns adds that he "moved his head."[11] Not only did *pîkahin okosisa* start to tell about the future (*ê-kiskiwêhikêt*), but he also preached. "He was sent back by God," Burns said, "by a higher power."[12]

Bill Stonestand said that, "as soon as he got up, he started preaching [to] his parents and friends, and . . . preaching about God."[13] He added, "They wanted to baptize all of the people," so they sent for a preacher south of Prince Albert. But two preachers came. One did not believe the story, but the other did. The one that did not believe the story died. Stonestand said the man was being punished.[14] He added:

> I am going to tell you what happened a long time [ago]. After he told his parents and people that the white man is going to be here, they going to shock the ground, with so many that is going to be here, but he said he didn't mind. He was happy. That was the way it was supposed to be.[15]

In addition to wanting to help people be baptized, and baptizing people himself, *pîkahin okosisa* prophesied many other things (*ê-kî-kiskiwêhikêt*). Charlie Burns said that *pîkahin okosisa* left his body and travelled:

> He said, "I was flying." He was flying around up there. And he seen this world, *tânisi ê-wî-ispayik,* what's going to happen in this world, in the future? It is going to be bad. And he seen . . . at that time there used to be, it was all bush . . . where Fort La Corne is, it was all bush. He said, "You are going to see the day that . . . something is going to be running around here. Red. And it is going to destroy all the bush." And then he said, "They are going to plant something here in this ground." And

he talked about the airplanes, flying around. "They'll be sending [machines] flying around here that . . . makes lots of noise, the motor."[15]

pîkahin okosisa said that families would split up more in the future. He spoke about the kind of houses we would live in. He also spoke of the hardships people would experience:

> He seen all that. That old man. And then he predicted what's happening . . . been happening, eh. He talked about the war, the First World War, the Second World War, he talked about that, he seen it. And what is going to happen in this reserve of ours. . . . He predicted that it is going to be bad: that people are going to fight over again. *ê-wî-nôtinitocik*. That's what he predicted.[16]

In another interview, Charlie Burns told me that people "*ê-wî-pakwâtitocik*" ("they will hate each other.")[17] Many who know the story believe this to be a forecast of the present turmoil, not only on the reserve but also in the world. *pîkahin okosisa* also talked about the future, *wî-âyimahk*,[18] about how there would be great fires in the northern skies.[19]

I have heard stories all my life that there would be a massive change in the world. People constantly talked about the coming hard times. Edward Caisse from Green Lake spoke about how we were going to go back to live as we had before, with no technology. For people of my father's age, the narrative of *pîkahin okosisa* must be understood as a function of this generational dynamic. During the massive changes around the Great Lakes area between 1806 and 1812, some spiritual leaders had preached that all "things white" should be thrown away, and that people should go back to their roots, to throw away technology.

My father also told me that *pîkahin okosisa* said, "My people will have good hunting near *mêskanaw*," which is a town in Saskatchewan relatively close to the James Smith Reserve. This part of the story points to the belief that the people of *cikâstêpêsin* would eventually get their land back.

According to Charlie Burns, my great-grandfather Abel McLeod was chief when our band sold *sôkâw-ministik* in 1948. My great-grandfather was the last traditionally appointed leader of the reserve, and widely respected. He was noted for giving food to the needy, which was certainly a prized Cree value. Everyone voted for the sale, and the people had enough money from it to live reasonably well for about two years. After hearing various aspects of this story, I believe that the island was sold for two reasons: because the people needed more food, and because there were bad feelings associated with the land because of the flood.

pîkahin okosisa lived for another week after coming back to life, and then he died for good:

> He slept on the ground, he wanted to . . . stay in his tipi every night. He wanted to sleep in the green grass all the time. And on the seventh day, he knew that there was one man that didn't like to go and pitch his tent [the tent of *pîkahin okosisa*] to where he wanted to sleep, eh. He got tired of changing his positions for sleeping. This one guy got tired of it and he told him that he wanted too much to be done. And then that old man knew. That night he told his son that. He told his son that one man here "One man here doesn't like me. So I'll be, I'll be gone tonight," he said. He said, "wait and I'll go away tonight." So he did. He died that night.[20]

One of *pîkahin okosisa's* predictions that all storytellers stress was *ê-wî-pôni-askîwik* — "the world will end." This is an aspect of the story that I have puzzled over. What does it mean? Does it mean that the traditional world of the Cree would end?

In Charlie Burns's understanding, he talks about Euro-Canadians destroying the world. He describes Euro-Canadians as *osâm iyinîsiw* — "too intelligent"[21] — but that the world would be cleansed and people would be reminded that the true power, the higher power, was God, not the technology that comes from Western culture. Charlie notes: "*môniyâw mistahi ê-iyinîsit* (the white is very intelligent), *kêkâc* (almost) as smart as God, but God is *maskawisîw* (strong)."[22] He says the reason *pîkahin okosisa* was sent back was "*ê-pê-wîhtamân ê-maskawisît manitow* (I come to tell that God is strong)."[23]

The late Bill Stonestand stressed the personal salvation aspect: the good news that *pîkahin okosisa* brought would help people survive the end of the world. He said that the devil would come and knock on the door, and when he comes, "if you don't have a Bible, you are going to fall down on the floor and die."[24] He encouraged people to "read the Bible, even a little bit,"[25] and was concerned about his grandchildren: "I would like to see my grandchildren and great-grandchildren go to church."[26]

pîkahin okosisa predicted that someone who was *ê-iyinîsit* would solve the problems of the reserve and bring the people back together. That person, to the best of my knowledge, has to yet appear.

The prophecy of someone bringing people help seems to give older people hope that the infighting that exists on our reserve will come to an end, and that we could move toward being a strong community again.

The story of *pîkahin okosisa* gave people hope at a time when all hope seemed to be fading. *pîkahin okosisa* took the ancient ways of the Cree people and layered them with Christianity. He provided his people with a pathway through which we could understand the world and make sense of it. I am truly grateful for having knowledge of this story. I have written it down so that people in the future will know about it.

CHAPTER EIGHT

EMBODIED MEMORY:
CONTEMPORARY CREE POLITICAL IDENTITY

IN THE PREVIOUS CHAPTERS, I have written about the disruption of Cree Indigenous memory. However, the oral history of Cree-speaking people still vividly holds their embodied experience, and many stories still tell of the massive changes that the Cree people have experienced.

As noted in chapter six, "Coming Home through Stories," the struggle to maintain Indigenous Cree memory is very possible in today's world. Not only can the narrative survive, but these narratives provide the basis for an anti-colonial political imagination that struggles to preserve the Indigenous political system and identity.

I had a grandfather, Gabriel Vandall, who was a distinguished war veteran. One of his grandfathers was *masaskêpiw*, older brother of *atâhkakohp* (Star-blanket). Within the Cree kinship system, that would also make *atâhkakohp*, too, his grandfather. His life story as a soldier is an interesting entry point to the ongoing narrative of the survival of Indigenous Cree political memory and action.

My father told me a story about this *mosôm* (grandfather), Gabriel Vandall, who was involved in the battle of D-Day in World War II:

When they had first come ashore and onto land at the event that has been called D-Day, they were standing on a large boat with his friends, this Gabe and his fellow trainees and one that he had trained with. They were standing there together looking and waiting to offload and the Germans [*sasâkisîwak*] were shooting at them from shore. While they were standing there together, him and his friend, his friend was hit with a bullet and his friend was hit in the neck and was decapitated. Immediately thereafter, Gabe was angry that his friend had been killed even before they were able to offload, it was like he was blinded with rage and he carried this feeling of rage with him from that moment that they offloaded over there all the way through until the fighting ended.[1]

My father and uncle were always welding and fixing things. While they were welding (*ispîhk ê-kî-akohkasikêcik*), they would often talk about *nimosôm* Gabriel. Apparently Gabriel had an idea to save lives in the tanks that involved welding:

> It was there when they landed on D-Day and they were fighting, they were small those things I don't know what they are called, like those tanks, American tanks, Sherman tanks those ones. Those that were in the back, the Germans had big bombs and when they were hit they immediately were destroyed when the bullets hit the tanks because the bullets were large and powerful, even when the Sherman tank was hit they would explode. He used to say, "It was because the metal used was too thin and the interior of the tank was also destroyed including the men that were housed inside," he used to say. Those that were sent to the front lines were worried because they knew that they would be killed, those that were inside the tanks. It came about that while he was helping he came up with an idea to put what a bulldozer has on its front, to weld a large bulldozer blade onto the tank and this is what would be hit when they were shot at, it would be the first thing that would be hit and damaged, this is what he helped with in coming up with this idea. This is what he and his friends came up with in building this but you will not hear of it spoken about anywhere. This is what I used to hear, he helped in coming up with this idea then.[2]

Gabriel was a Cree-speaking man who lived near the *yêkawiskâwikamâhk* (Sandy Lake) Reserve in north-central Saskatchewan. Another important layer of his story is the fact that one of his uncles, Joseph Vandall, is buried outside the graveyard at Batoche. Joseph Vandall's grandfather, in turn, had been a general in Napoleon's army.

There is an ironic twist in the fact that some of his ancestors had fought against the British Empire, but he himself fought for Canada, a former member and now an ally of that same empire, in two World Wars. His experience as a soldier included the Battle of Juno Beach, June 6, 1944. His experience was profoundly physical, profoundly visceral, completely embodied. As anti-colonial thinker Frantz Fanon suggested in *The Wretched of the Earth*, the experience of colonialism is essentially one of the body; we hold these experiences within us and pass this embodied memory through the generations.

An interesting story I heard from the Métis author Maria Campbell was about our grandmother, *cîhcam*. *cîhcam* was Gabriel's mother. Campbell told me that *cîhcam* had the *nôtokwêw âtayôhkan* lodge (Grandmother Spirit Lodge). She did not take treaty and lived in what is today the Prince Albert National Park. During the time of the oppression of Indigenous ceremonies, she used to have her sweat lodge under the kitchen table. She would put a blanket over the table and put a skillet with small, heated rocks in it on the floor. She would then conduct her ceremony.

cîhcam lived off the land despite the fact that her uncle, *atâhkakohp*, was one of the most prominent leaders in her territory. Interestingly enough, Earth Woman, a daughter of Big Bear, also did not take treaty, and lived her life at *manitow sâkahikan* (near Neilburg, Saskatchewan).

Gabriel's people, my people, carried the embodied memory of being torn from our homeland, and a violent encounter with the British memory, yet we held on to an ancient memory. *mosôm* Gabriel came from a family full of stories with strong connections to the land, but I have often wondered why my grandfather fought for Canada when the same country had treated him and our family so badly. What inspired him to fight for a nation that did not recognize his rights as an Indigenous person?

Part of the answer lies in the military traditions of the family. *mosôm's* ancestors were soldiers, and so was he. Yet the answer also lies deeper, I think: in his actions as a decorated soldier, he was seeking a dignity and recognition not available to him in his own country.

Gabriel earned many medals, which he hung on his wall. He was honoured when he passed away in 1966. My uncle Burton Vandall told me, "The military buried him and many military personnel came when he passed away and they buried him, he was buried in that way. . . . Over there in *yêkawiskâwikamâhk* [Sandy Lake] there, he was buried there that one. That is probably why his siblings are buried there also."[3] He was honoured by the army, like many other First Nations veterans. All of these heroes were trying to find their place in a radically transformed world. They were trying to find honour and respect.

Another grandfather of mine, the late John R. McLeod, suffered many of the indignities of colonialism, including residential school. Despite this, he held on to an older memory that helped him place himself in the world, and helped place himself in history. He saw that narratives needed a political structure to give them reality, to give them more embodiment. For *nimosôm,* this political structuring involved immersing himself in a historical understanding of the treaties.

In 1976, John R. McLeod was chairperson of the centennial commemoration. He was part of the first wave of urbanized Cree in the late 1960s, and one member of a group of Cree people participating in the larger Canadian society. Despite this connection and the opportunities afforded him and his family, he emphasized that the treaties were the basis for the survival of the Cree people:

> Our elders tell us that the reason our people and our leaders went to Fort Carlton was to work for the survival of Indian people. One hundred years ago, they called upon the Queen to send her representations. One hundred years ago, they met with the commissioners and negotiated a Treaty which allowed the Indian people to survive as Indians, and which allowed us to be here as Indians today and whatever the federal government or anyone else may say, without the efforts of our forefathers at Fort Carlton and Fort Pitt, we would not exist as Indians today.[4]

My grandfather had experienced the process of colonization first-hand — the attempt to strip the identity from his soul. This process had made him sick, had taken life from him, and had become embodied in his life. Colonized peoples embody this experience, and it often affects their physical being.

There was a long period in which the Cree and the Europeans had engaged in mutually beneficial trade. J. E. Foster characterizes this as a compact, a relationship between equals.[5] The relationship eventually changed to one of subservience through the imposition of the *Indian Act* and the failure of the government to honour the treaties. The treaties, of course, were an embodiment of a relationship between equals.

It is worthwhile to reflect on the dynamics of the relationship between Indigenous nations and empires. Sometimes the period between initial contact and pressure from the colonizer to surrender land is long; at other times, when the colonizer comes as a conqueror, there is no distance at all. For the Cree, the difference between these two points was very long, which I think informs the relationship. Because of the longstanding relationship between Europeans and the *nêhiyawak*, there was a process of treaty making, which in some ways mimicked the activity and processes of the fur trade.

As noted in previous chapters, throughout the 1870s and 1880s, Cree people were in transition. Treaties were being made and the Cree were trying to adapt to shifting circumstances. The federal government's agricultural policy was not working, however; there were not adequate implements, and food was withheld. During this period, *mistahi-maskwa,* Big Bear, was trying to organize the people and negotiate better treaty terms. He attempted to use his waning influence over the young men to refrain from taking violent action, as he knew the repercussions would be extreme. Eventually, he surrendered at Fort Carlton with his son, *mistatim-awâsis.*

ê-mâyahkamikahk — "where it went wrong," the events of 1885, including the violence — ended the possibility of intercultural dialogue and any meaningful notion of citizenship for Indigenous people within Canada, for dialogue is only possible when there is respect and open-mindedness. *ê-mâyahkamikahk* also effectively enabled the government to bring to an end any possibility of re-opening treaty discussions, as by that time most First Nations leaders were dead, in prison, or in exile.

A story I heard many years ago from Violet Coleman, whose grandparents came from Lipton, Saskatchewan, involves her grandparents, Thomas and Harriet Anne Murray (née Wannamaker). They were originally from Ontario and were among the first farmers in the area. He was the mayor, and also sat on the school board. Violet spoke of how the Mounties went to the door of her grandparents' house and asked for food. Big Bear was shackled to a wagon on his way to Stoney Mountain penitentiary. Her grandmother asked about Big Bear. "Forget him," she was told. "But if you are hungry then he is probably hungry too." She brought tea and food on plates for *mistahi-maskwa,* and fed him along with the others. She fed *mistahi-maskwa* first, however. This story shows that not everyone in English-speaking society was against *mistahi-maskwa.* Some recognized his humanity and tried to help him. It speaks to the way conversation can exist in inter-ethnic relations. Often the paradigm of conversation, of the recognition of yourself and of common humanity, is lost in the study of the history of Indigenous people.

After 1885, the pass system was imposed, various Cree and Métis leaders were imprisoned, and relations between Indigenous people and the newcomers entered a new era. The terms and ideals of the treaties were superseded by the imperatives of colonialism and the *Indian Act*.

The federal government continued to develop the reserve system, severely restricting Indigenous people to their assigned territories. The reserve system and the *Indian Act* caused a shift in the economy, changes in language to some extent through residential schools, the imposition of an alien political structure, and the undermining of traditional spirituality as Canada tried to impose cultural hegemony.

Although Canada was a multi-ethnic state, cultural and political hegemony was constructed on the basis of the English language and British political structures. While the state has been made to appear neutral and liberal, in the classic sense, the political and cultural foundations of this country are European. What has been "dressed-up" as universalism is simply an element of colonialism.

The League of Indians

The period from 1885 to the First World War was one of relative political inactivity for the *nêhiyawak*. Many people were simply in survival mode, dealing with mainstream culture and the continual erosion of their land base. But there were still elders who could remember in precise detail the time before the reserve period; these keepers of ancestral memory refused to be overwhelmed and sought younger people to hold and pass on the ancient memory.

Because of the war and the experiences many people in the armed forces had of being treated equally, and learning to speak English in residential schools, a new generation of leaders emerged. The war instilled in people the notion that they were part of the country, and in warfare they had proven themselves as equals. They could then, in turn, make compelling arguments to be treated with dignity and accorded the privileges of citizenship which had been denied them. Being treated with dignity and respect in the army inspired many Cree people to seek a more inclusive notion of citizenship. At the same time, they wanted to protect their treaty rights and maintain their status as a separate nation.

As I learned through the stories of the late John B. Tootoosis and my great-grandfather Abel McLeod, there was a great irony embodied in the residential school system: it taught young Indigenous people to read the *Indian Act* and letters from the government for themselves, allowing them subsequently to ask questions and challenge governmental officials directly.

The League of Indians arose during this period after the First World War. People were concerned with maintaining the treaties, but also determined to achieve fuller participation in mainstream society, especially in the fields of education and health.

F. O. Loft, a veteran of the First World War and a Mohawk from the Six Nations Reserve in Ontario, began to organize Indigenous people on a national scale. His efforts can be seen as an extension of *mistahi-maskwa*'s attempts to organize on a regional scale. Loft attempted to create a pan-Indian nationalism, constantly referred to the nationhood of Indigenous people, and protested the patronizing and oppressive *Indian Act*, as well as other coërcive policies.

In the west, this cause was taken up by Edward Ahenakew, who was active in the League of Indians. He was also an Anglican priest, and protested the treatment of children in residential schools and sought better conditions for his people. Yet Ahenakew, like many others in the movement, was cautious about voting in federal elections. He and others thought it might limit their treaty rights; by voting, Indian political structures would be undermined.

Conference of the League of Indians of Western Canada,
Thunderchild Reserve, Saskatchewan (Glenbow Archives, NA-928-1),

John B. Tootoosis noted how the church tried to cripple Indigenous identity:

> The Church discouraged Indians from joining the organization [the League of Indians of Western Canada]. The nuns would lecture the Indians. They would tell the children everyday that if they listened to their parents they would go to hell. After many years of this the young children didn't listen to their parents. They were brainwashed. They created a conflict inside every tipi on the reservation. The church cut off the very people [the elders] who should have been teaching and preaching and guiding the young people.[6]

Attempts were made by various political organizations, including the Allied Bands (later called the Protective Association for the Indians and their treaties) north of Regina, to close the residential schools. The organization sought to strive for a better Indian education with schools on every reserve in order to bring Indians a better standard of socio-economic development.[7] The League of Indians of Western Canada, an offshoot of Loft's organization, was also against the schools: "The League opposed residential schools — the church wanted to dominate the people through the schools."[8] Tootoosis was the grandson of

Edward Ahenakew (centre front) with the League of Indians
(Saskatchewan Archives Board, RA-10196).

osâwâw-askiy-akohp (Yellow Mud Blanket), who was the elder brother of Chief Poundmaker (*pîhtokahânapiwiyin*). Tootoosis rose to prominence when he became leader of the League of Indians of Western Canada after Edward Ahenakew stepped down in the 1920s because of pressure from the church. He later became the first president of the Federation of Saskatchewan Indians in 1958.

Tootoosis commented that "The Church was supporting the domination. They were doing the brainwashing in those residential schools. . . . I went through the mill myself. I saw what was happening and what they were trying to do."[9] According to my father, John Tootoosis maintained that one had to be careful about one's involvement in white religious groups, because there was always the danger of them using their power to dominate Indian politics.

Tootoosis often spoke of how hard it was to organize people, because "Indians weren't organized before. They were so damn dominated by the government."[10] With so little control over their lives, people were seemingly unable to make decisions, but as they became organized in the 1920s and 1930s, they began to break the yoke of domination. A fundamental demand of Indian political organizations in that period was to end the domination of the residential schools. "The League opposed residential schools," Tootoosis said, but "the church wanted to dominate the people and keep the schools."[11]

In many ways, John Tootoosis was the *mistahi-maskwa* of the 20th century. He struggled to maintain *nêhiyawak* identity in a difficult time, and led the movement to regain our rights and assert our dignity as a people. He did this through his stories, his connection to place, and the help of his father. As his biographers write, "John Tootoosis, Sr. would not allow his sons to feel rejected and useless. This perceptive man had encouraged all his children from their earlier years to listen to the Elders in Council and then debate on the various matters that had been under discussion with one another."[12] While there were severe pressures on *nêhiyawak* at that time, people found ways to preserve their identity and their place in the world. Stories and language led some back to their true identities.

John Tootoosis was trying to protect "Cree space" — both the spiritual and physical home of the Cree. "Cree space" could be understood as a metaphorical way of describing the narratives, the land, and all the things that allow the *nêhiyawak* to express themselves in relation to their ancestors.

The late Wilfred Tootoosis, John's oldest son, reflected on his experiences in residential school and how he was singled out because of his father's activities:

I had quite an experience in school. I'd get picked on. The nuns and priests spoke against my dad's movement, everywhere, in church, in the classroom. And when somebody did something wrong they ganged up and blamed me for it. . . . They could have had my dad shot if they had a chance to.[13]

The children of activists and spiritual leaders were often hit hardest, and were singled out and attacked regularly. My father told me that the priests used to refer to John Tootoosis's children as "communists."

There are many stories about John Tootoosis and his struggle for the rights of the Cree people. Here is one I heard from Pat Cayen from Muskeg Lake:

The Tootoosis family at one time had only one saddle. John's sons would use the saddle to ride, an activity they enjoyed very much. However, one time there was a man from Cold Lake who was visiting. He had ridden a horse all of the way from Cold Lake to Poundmaker, which is a considerable distance. John had pity on him and gave him the saddle so that his trip would be better because the man from Cold Lake still had to travel to the proximity of Regina. Some time later John was in Cold Lake at a meeting. He was sitting at a table when the man who was given the saddle approached him. He looked at John as though he recognized him. Finally, he did recognize him and started to talk to John. He learned that John did not have very much money to travel back, so he gave John $15, which was a lot of money back then.[14]

In the early days of Indian organization, people would help each other, stay at each other's houses and feed travellers. They would share what little they had and collect money to help activists attend meetings. Leaders back then had a lot of support because they truly did represent the people. My father said once how people would share hay with one another and extra things with those who didn't quite have enough.

The League continued to operate in Cree territory alongside other organizations. Finally, in 1946, the Union of Saskatchewan Indians was organized at the Barry Hotel in Saskatoon. Various groups merged to form the larger organization. In the document describing this meeting, there are two seemingly conflicting strands of narrative, one stressing a sense of nationalism, of treaty, and justice, the other stressing universalism. "The Union shall be democratic and non sectarian" and "promoting respect and tolerance for all."[15]

Joe Dreaver, grandson of *mistawâsis* (Big Child) and a World War II veteran, noted:

> The Indian Department has gone to work without consulting the Indians; they never asked us where our grievances might originate. This is not the treaty. Years ago a nation made a treaty with the English crown, but the *Indian Act* was passed without our consent and it abrogates the treaty. They have done a great deal to improve our lot. But in Ottawa, they do not want us to organize. Are we living under democratic rule?[16]

As a veteran, he wanted some of the benefits of citizenship. He also wanted to protect the treaties, which he saw as the foundation for ensuring that his people were treated justly.

The Creation of Modern Indigenous Institutions

The resistance of various leaders such as John Tootoosis made the creation of modern institutions possible. An important aspect of *nêhiyâwiwin* and modernity is the strength with which the *nêhiyawak* opposed colonialism. Once the *nêhiyawak* began to control their own lives, the challenge became how to create new institutions. Things began to change as Indian people asserted their right to control their educational institutions. The late Smith Atimoyoo, the first director of the Saskatchewan Indian Cultural College, stressed the importance of knowing who we are: "It is very important that we, as Indian people, realize that we must learn to know who we are and what we should be doing."[17]

One of the most interesting recent developments has been the use of education to preserve culture. Instead of destroying culture, as in residential schools, education today has the capacity to strengthen it. It can also allow people to think outside modernity.

For example, the Blue Quill residential school in Saskatchewan was taken over in 1970 by the *nêhiyawak*. An untitled document of the Blue Quills Native Education Council states:

> We have to realize that we must take part in planning and in carrying out those plans if we are ever to regain our proper place in the social life of our country. We can no longer be content to let others do our think-

ing for us. We, ourselves, must take the action which will remove the discrepancies which have existed in education for Indians in the past.[18]

A 1972 National Indian Brotherhood position paper stressed the importance of children learning about their past, thus linking history, education, and self-government: "Unless a child learns about the forces which shape him: the history of his people, their values and customs, their language, he will never really know himself or his potential as a human being."[19] A new curriculum was needed:

> The present schools system is culturally alien to native students. Where the Indian contribution is not entirely ignored, it is often cast in unfavourable light. School curricula in federal and provincial schools should recognize Indian culture, values, customs, languages and the Indian contribution to Canadian development.[20]

Jean Barman, Yvonne Hébert, and Don McCaskill observe that Indian control of Indian education is founded on two principles: "parental responsibility and local responsibility."[21]

In Saskatchewan, attempts were made to develop curricula that would help foster the retention of Aboriginal languages. The Cree Language Committee attempted to implement a meaningful curriculum in the schools. Language was stressed because it was seen as a valuable source of cultural preservation: "We also feel that learning of Cree is important for our children. Their ability to appreciate the history and mode of living of their people depends considerably on their knowledge of our language."[22] Indian control of Indian education would "ensure the transmission of Indian values, identity, and tradition while providing a quality education."[23] Following centuries of domination and the imposition of alien values, Indigenous people are reaffirming the validity of their own cultures; they are redefining political, economic, and social priorities in the context of the late 20th and early 21st centuries. Control over education lies at the heart of this process.[24]

An example of the *nêhiyawak* attempting to gain control of our institutions occurred in 1973 on the James Smith Reserve. It was called the "louse incident." Children who were bussed into the nearby town of Kinistino for school were wrongfully accused of having lice. The incident was painful for the children, but it energized the people of the reserve to establish their own school. A news report of the time described the louse incident as the "final straw that capped a growing disenchantment by both parents and the white man's school."[25] The Kinistino school had received federal funding, but as Noel Dyck and John McLeod write, "over a period of fifteen years these schools were unable and perhaps even unwilling to meet the needs of the students from James Smith, even though they received large amounts of money in tuition and capital agreements."[26]

The establishment of a Cree-controlled school on the reserve was the first step toward self-government. By controlling schools, people could begin to reverse colonialism and establish Indigenous institutions founded on Indigenous philosophy. Robert Regnier, a former employee of the Saskatchewan Indian Cultural College and a friend of *nimosôm*, shared the following story with me concerning the louse incident:

> The events had reached a climax, and there was a meeting where representatives of Indian Affairs came. Before that meeting, the school committee had got together and created stereotypes of different officials from Indian Affairs; there was "the know it all," for example. The school committee created hypothetical questions that these people would have to answer. For instance, they practised how they would respond to the question, "You will not be able to do this. How can you take over the school?"[27]

The point of the story is that mainstream institutions and their representatives were still patronizing toward Indigenous people.

Eventually my community acquired control over the school and developed programs. Language lessons were created and some wanted to use land claims research to develop histories. John Tobias commented that the information could be made to be part of a social studies program.[28]

The James Smith Reserve was the first in Saskatchewan to establish educational control. Two years after my reserve achieved control over schooling, my grandfather became the chairperson of the centennial commemorations of Treaty 6. At a meeting in 1975, the minutes read: "Mr. McLeod expresses his happiness every time a new school is opened on a reserve but he wishes to see more of the Indian image projected from these schools."[29] A survivor of the residential schools, *mosôm's* vision was:

> We should realize that it is up to us to teach our children their history and make them proud to be Indians. There is a quote which reads: The

public school is a state institution created by the state for its own preservation. Every reserve is a state and so should we Indians rely on our own people to preserve our own culture by teaching our children.[30]

By articulating Cree history and culture in the schools, the *nêhiyawak* would achieve self-government because we would know who we were as a people. In a later meeting, *nimosôm* stated, "The reserve is also an institution, an Indian institution where children can be taught their Indian history and language and be proud that they are Indians."[31] My *mosôm* wanted us to be able to draw upon our collective narrative memory in contemporary times.

nimosôm used to ask fundamental questions about contemporary life, such as, "What have we given up in exchange for the modern life?" and, "What stories have we forgotten in order to live in today's world?" In 1976, he wondered about the changes that had occurred over the past 100 years:

And we have wondered what our ancestors would say to us if they could be with us today. I, myself, often wonder about some of the things I have done in my lifetime. I have broken and worked down 400 acres of land on James Smith. What would a man from 1876 or 1776 or even further back say to me, to all of us, if he were here today?[32] . . . Have we exchanged the buffalo for welfare payments? Have we traded our own religion for the white man's churches? Our medicine for his? Indian languages for English?[33]

I return to the question, "What motivated my grandfather Gabriel Vandall to fight for Canada during the Second World War?" I believe he was profoundly motivated by experiencing the embodiment of colonialism, and also from being taken away from an Indigenous relationship to the land. Perhaps, paradoxically, he joined the army not to fight for Queen and country, but for his dignity and respect. He fought to find meaning in the world, and to shape his life with narrative and story. Having experienced profound political and spiritual turmoil, soldiering allowed him to connect to an embodied past, to an embodied experience.

My grandfather John R. McLeod was motivated by slightly different reasons. He, also, had experienced the brutalizing effects of colonization; he had attended the residential school at Gordon's and endured a great deal of hardship there. Despite this — or more probably because of it — he was profoundly motivated to maintain the Cree language and a distinctive political identity. Narrative memory connects us to the past, but the memory is also embodied in the land and in our bodies. Through the lives of two of my grandfathers, I can see their struggle to find meaning in the world as a reaction to colonization, and as a means of bringing the past to the present.

One cannot maintain a distinct identity without knowing the past; one will simply have a distorted sense of one's place in the world, shifted and transformed by a colonized understanding of the world wherein the memories and narratives of ancient ancestors are shrouded. Both my grandfathers, in their own ways, embodied this memory in their actions and deeds.

CHAPTER NINE

CREE NARRATIVE IMAGINATION

kawâhkatos WAS A LEADER AT A CROSSROADS IN HISTORY. The world of the Cree in western Canada was changing rapidly. The buffalo were retreating into the ground (*kotâwîwak*) and into the water (*ê-mistâpâwêhisocik*). The expansion of the British Empire was forcing an economic shift from hunting to farming. A Cree chief from the Treaty 4 area, *kawâhkatos* listened to the Queen's representative and imagined another possibility, grounded in ancient Cree narrative memory:

> One of the Queen's representatives had come to negotiate with the In-dians. His aides treated him grandly and even had a chair for him to sit on. A cloth was spread on the ground and several bags of money were placed on it. The representative explained through an interpreter how many bags of money the Queen had sent. [A Chief] was told this and said, "Tell the Queen's representative to empty the money and fill the bags with dirt. Tell him to take the bags back to England to the Queen. She has paid for that much land."[1]

Cree narrative imagination is another aspect of Cree narrative memory: it is a way of drawing upon the past and the present and projecting these elements

into the future. Cree narrative imagination is overtly futuristic in its orienta-
tion, which is embodied within our lives and bodies, and can reshape our social
space. It is quintessentially an Indigenous conception and practice of theory.
In the case of *kawâhkatos*, he imagined a space where the Cree would maintain
their independence and attachment to the land and the powers of the land.

nêhiyawêwin means "Cree language" at a literal level, but if one examines
the root of the word it really means "Cree sound" — the "*-wê*" stem denoting
sound. This stem is found at the end of many names: *manitowêw* (Almighty
Voice), *mistanaskowêw* (Calling Badger), or *kâ-kisîwêw* (Loud Voice). All
these names hold stories — stories of struggle and attempts to hold onto Cree
culture. *manitowêw* killed a cow in order to feed his family, and then spent
two years evading the authorities. *mistanaskowêw* was taught Cree syllabics by
the Creator because he was told that the Cree language would be threatened
in the future. *kâ-kisîwêw*, like *kawâhkatos*, questioned the transfer of land
from the Hudson's Bay Company to the Dominion of Canada. All these men
tried to preserve Cree culture; their names bore sound, and they struggled to
preserve the Cree presence in the landscape of sound.

Various storytellers have linked me to the past; through them I have learned
narratives of past days and narratives about my ancestors and about places
that are important to the Cree people. Names, places, and stories ground a
people in the world. They give a people a narrative structure to organize their
experience, and through which they can link to the past.

Part of the act of narrative imagination involves dwelling in the visceral,
nuanced sound landscape of our childhoods. Kiowa author N. Scott Momaday writes:

> . . . the sound is like a warm wind that arises from my childhood. It
> is the music of memory. I have come to know that much of the power
> and magic and beauty of words consist not in meaning but in sound.
> Storytellers, actors and children know this, too.[2]

> My father told me stories from Kiowa oral tradition even before I could
> talk. Those stories became permanent in my mind, the nourishment
> of my imagination for the whole of my life. They are among the most
> valuable gifts that I have ever been given.[3]

The stories form both the basis of his identity and the way he relates to the
world, the way in which he threads his experiences together.

Modernity and Colonialism:
Dislocation from Collective Sound and Memory

Cree narrative memory is embodied and reflective. It allows us to think critically about the world around us through stories and through the process of
trying to imagine new stories that we could collectively and individually live
through.

Cree culture consists of several influences and naturally has changed over
time. It is open-ended and multi-layered; I have used the paradigm of narrative to characterize this process. Cree narrative memory is an ongoing conversation, a constant play between present, past, and future. Participants in this
conversation have spoken many languages and have had a variety of ways of
seeing the world. However, the Cree language and traditions are the threads
that hold this particular fabric together.

Many stories reflect on the importance of language. The loss of language
is one facet of the process I have called spiritual exile. Harry Blackbird, an
elder from the Meadow Lake area, told about a man visited by his deceased
wife. She told him about the passing of a young boy. The story reflects on the
struggle to preserve the Cree language:

> Upon entering the spirit world he was greeted by an *oskâpêwis* [an elder's
> helper or apprentice] who led the young man down an easy road to fol-
> low. At a certain point, the road forked going in two directions. They first
> travelled down the road to the right. This road was also easy to follow.
>
> The young people then began to speak in the language of his ances-
> try — *nêhiyawêwin*. Unfortunately, the young man could not make
> out what they were saying even though he was of the same nation . . .
> *nêhiyaw*. He even had the two long braids of hair, common trademarks
> for *nêhiyawak* who were following the *nêhiyâwiwin* way. Confused and
> feeling lost, the young man was quickly whisked away by the *oskâpêwis*
> towards the other.[4]

Maria Campbell also discussed the experience of spiritual exile, the conflict
between the modern world and the traditional, Cree-speaking world. It is
her relationship with her great-grandmother Cheechum (*cîhcam*, who is also
my grandmother) that furnishes her with stories that guide her through her
life. Once she spent the whole day with her grandmother, who gave her the
following advice:

Now I know that you belong to me. Don't let anyone tell you that any-thing is impossible, because if you believe honestly in your heart that there's something better for you, then it will all come true. Go out there and find what you want and take it, but always remember who you are and why you want it.[5]

The stories of our grandmother have grounded her and have provided a map by which she can negotiate her way. *cîhcam's* uncle was *atâhkakohp*, a leading chief of Treaty 6, whose son was Gabriel Vandall, a distinguished veteran of World War I and World War II.

Edward Ahenakew, a Cree priest from the Sandy Lake Reserve in north central Saskatchewan, also lived part of his life in exile. The effects of reserve life were too severe, and Old Man Kiyâm had given up. Old Man Kiyâm, Ahenakew's semi-autobiographical character, was the first generation to expe-rience the exile of early reserve life. In order to deal with it, he tried to find a "home" in the white man's world, yet he failed. "In his youth he had tried to fit himself to the new ways; he thought that he would conquer; and he was defeated instead."[6] Ahenakew describes the conflict between the two different "locations" Old Man Kiyâm tried to straddle: "His own words, his own ac-count of a progressive reserve, had worked Old Kiyâm to great excitement, or else it was the remembrance of his own lost days and opportunity."[7] Old Man Kiyâm's embodied reality was an example of the historical manifestation of *ê-mâyahkamikahk*. The events of 1885 and the early reserve period led to the loss of Indigenous people's freedom, and, by extension, the loss of their place in the new world.

Yet, in his alleged failure, Old Man Kiyâm tries to find his way home through storytelling. He "reverted to the old Indian way of life, allowed his hair to grow long, and he chose to wander from house to house, reciting old legends, winning a reputation for himself as a storyteller."[8] His words echoed eternity. Jim Kâ-Nîpitêhtêw, an elder from Onion Lake, notes: "It's only the elders who have long since gone that speak through them. It's an echo of a wonderful life long ago."[9] It is the voices and wisdom of the old ones that guide us.

All the examples discussed point to the challenges of trying to live in the modern world, drawing upon the knowledge of our ancestors and trying to meet the struggles and challenges of today. Part of this involves seeing culture as a fluid, organic process. This goes against an essentialist conception of cul-ture.

Narrative Imagination:
Bridging Past, Present, and Future through *âtayôhkêwina*

One of the chief struggles of Cree narrative imagination is the discordance between the ancient memory that is embodied in our lives and our physical being, and the experience of modernity and colonialism. Often, these two sets of narratives and embodied ways of understanding the world have been in conflict. The use of *âtayôhkêwina* — sacred stories, or spiritual history, as one elder has described it — is one source of conceiving of a Cree critical theory, a narrative embodiment that creatively reflects on the situation and the world in which we find ourselves.

A central task of Cree narrative memory is to rethink the limitations of colonialism and the impositions of the mainstream culture. It is this dynamic element that makes it narrative memory. The attempt to discern the limitations of modernity from an Indigenous perspective has been called "trickster hermeneutics" by Gerald Vizenor.[10]

While helpful to some extent, Vizenor's notion relies on Western literary theory and distorts Indigenous narrative in some ways. The link between hermeneutics and Indigenous narrative realities contributes to transcultural dialogue, but it also distorts Indigenous narrative reality through the insistence of the term "trickster." The term is inaccurate.

The proper term is *kistêsinaw*, which denotes the notion of the elder brother. This instantly assumes a state of kinship and relationship between humans and the rest of creation. It also moves beyond the intersubjective limitations of human-based discourse which has dominated the West. It moves beyond the conceptual straitjacket that the term "trickster" puts *wîsahkêcâhk* in: the term suggests to some that this sacred being is little more than a buffoon. The concepts centred on the word in English include such words as "trickery," "tricky," and "trick," which indicate something less than the truth. One could argue that this is part of the same dynamic that exists when courts and governments have argued that Indigenous lands have been historically empty of laws and governance structures (the notion of *terra nullius*). The term "trickster" is part of this same trickery, making Indigenous narratives conceptually empty and potentially devoid of truth.

The narratives of *wîsahkêcâhk* should be seen as part of the *genre* of sacred stories, *âtayôhkêwina*. The term *âtayôhkêwina* denotes stories of *wîsahkêcâhk* (and, indeed, other beings). When we shift the paradigm to think of *âtayôhkêwina* as "spiritual narratives," we can see them as core to Cree culture and beliefs. They are key to the construction of what is meant by Cree narrative memory, and also Cree narrative imagination, which is essentially the process of expanding our narrative memory in light of new experiences. These narratives re-imagine the landscape of Cree territory, noting the place-names of *wîsahkêcâhk's* travels. The narratives also point to relationships between humans and other beings, and to the possibility of radically re-imagining constructed social spaces.

Indigenous Theory

Many people have attempted to articulate Indigenous models of theory. One way is to conceive of it as a philosophical activity of reflective consciousness and an activity of thinking outside a state of affairs in the world. One could also argue that the aim of Cree philosophy to think beyond colonial barriers is a theoretical activity. Others may say that "theory" is an inherently Western idea and cannot be rendered within Indigenous philosophies, or that there is no need for a discussion of Indigenous theory or philosophy.

Cree narrative imagination is one way of conceiving Indigenous theory. It is a visionary process of imagining another state of affairs. This does not imply that one is seeking Utopia; one is simply seeking a different possibility, trying to conceive of a different way in which people might live together. Big Bear, *mistahi-maskwa, kâ-kî-itiht* (the one who was called), is an example of this, in that he struggled to maintain Cree independence against overwhelming odds. The late John Tootoosis is another example of a person embodying Cree narrative imagination. He imagined a condition, and sought a possibility whereby Indian people would not be dominated by the *Indian Act* and a system that was designed to destroy our identity and political institutions.

While there are important differences between how modernity has been experienced by Indigenous peoples such as the Cree, and by European nations, there are also important similarities. The German philosopher Martin Heidegger (1889–1976) offers insights into how modernity has transformed human consciousness. In his writings, Heidegger warned against the dangers of modern technology, for he thought it had the potential to overwhelm humanity. Initially, technology helped humans, but humans themselves eventually become tools of technology. In other words, the essence of humanity would be transformed by modern technology.[11]

In the spirit of *mistahi-maskwa*, we must struggle to regain our freedom on both the existential and the historical level. We must attempt to dream and have visions. Without dreams and idealism, we will truly be a conquered people. But, with vision, we may offer ourselves and the rest of the world solutions to the crisis of the modern age. We will rethink liberalism and democracy on the basis of our collective, lived experience.

Cree narrative memory has many levels and aspects, and conforms to Bahktin's notion of dialogism:

> Dialogism is the characteristic epistemological mode of a world dominated by heteroglossia: this means that the societal dialogue involves more than one voice, and there is not one dominant narrative, one metanarrative. Everything means, is understood, as a part of a greater whole — there is a constant interaction between meanings, all of which have the potential of conditioning others.[12]

Many old Cree storytellers were aware of this state within *nêhiyawêwin.* They would speak of how one could tell *wîsahkêcâhk* stories until one was white in the hair, and even then there would be more stories. There is always an abundance of narrative voices regarding the elder brother/transformer, because in essence he is only limited by the imagination of those who participate in Cree culture. With regard to *wîsahkêcâhk*, there are many voices and many perspectives. One could argue that the elder brother/transformer himself/herself creates a state of heteroglossia through the questioning of social space.

Dialogue and Poetry: A Paradigm for Indigenous Theory

The old people at the time of treaties were thinking ahead to the future, *ôtê nîkân.* They were thinking about how their children would live in the future. Some, like *mistahi-maskwa,* raised the questions that Chipmunk raised about whether what the Queen was offering could replace *kâ-miyikowisiyahk* (what the Creator has given us). They thought ahead and wanted to make sure their descendents would have a way of making a living. *kawâhkatos* also pointed to this general concern.

Great stories challenge the status quo. They challenge the social space around us, and the way society structures the world. Great stories urge us to rethink that social space. Great storytellers are embodiments of the social climate around them. Through storytelling, they are able to question the world around us. They are able to question the injustices that are often inflicted on them. Storytelling is a subversive act that causes people to question the society around them. Storytellers hold the core of a counter memory, and offer another political possibility.

Storytellers have to remember the past, and they have to remember the language. They have to remember the stories that made their ancestors the people they were. Their bodies become houses of ancient sound. But storytellers also have a responsibility to the future. They have a responsibility to imagine a different world, where Cree stories will thrive, but also wherein the social space will be just. One of the central tasks of great storytellers is what I call narrative imagination.

In Saskatchewan, our numbers are rapidly increasing and we are starting to feel our strength. We have to ask ourselves fundamental questions about the nature of our relationship with the rest of society. We must ask ourselves about the direction we are going, and what we have to do to survive as Indigenous people.

As Indigenous people, we are attempting to revive our modes of being. Clearly, the revitalization of Indigenous cultures involves an array of people, from political leaders to religious leaders, educators, academics, writers, and artists.

The survival of the Cree people depends on the creative powers found within the collective narrative imagination. It is through drawing on the best of our past traditions and the embodiment of contemporary experiences that we can move toward a dynamic future. This has organically happened in the past — the horse, syllabics, Christianity, farming — but the adaptation of new elements has always been in relation to older ones.

Cree narrative imagination can be best articulated by the Cree term *mamâhtâwisiwin*, which could perhaps be best translated as "tapping into the Great Mystery," or "tapping into the Life Force." The term used to describe the elder Brother *wîsahkêcâhk, ê-mamâhtâwisit,* was also used to describe *mistahi-maskwa*. All these beings struggled to move beyond the ordinary, and to rethink the space and world around them.

APPENDIX A

CREE GLOSSARY

NOTE: Cree alphabetization, dealing as it does with long and short vowels, is somewhat different than English. Short vowels precede long ones, and so the Cree alphabet reads: a, â, c, ê, h, i, î, k, m, n, o, ô, p, s, t, w, y. Also, a space or a hyphen outranks all letters — so, for instance, a prefix such as *kâ-* will form its own section of entries, with all words beginning *kâ-* grouped together, before moving on to other words such as *kâkikê.*

asiniy-kâpaw: Stonestand; Saulteaux man from Nut Lake; Grandfather of Clifford Sanderson.

askîhkân: reserve; literally, "fake land."

asotamâkê: make a promise that cannot be broken.

asotamâkêwin: a promise that cannot be broken.

atâhkakohp: Starblanket from the House People; not to be confused with the southern Cree leader whose name, while translated the same, is different in Cree: *acâhkosa kâ-otakohpit* (literally, "one who has stars for a blanket").

âmow-piyêsîs: humming bird; literally, "bee-bird."

âtayôhkan, âtayôhkanak: Spirit Being(s), sometimes translated as "grandfather(s)" or "grandmother(s)."

âtayôhkêwina: spiritual history, sometimes translated "sacred stories" or "legends."

âyimisîs: literally, "the little difficult one"; Big Bear's son.

cikâstêpêsin: Shadow on the Water; Cree chief.

cîhcam: daughter of *masaskêpiw;* niece of *atâhkakohp;* my great-great-great grandmother.

ê-iyinîsit: he is intelligent.

ê-kiskiwêhikêt: he prophesies.

ê-kî-âhkosit: he was sick.

ê-kî-kiskiwêhikêt: he prophesied.

ê-kî-mistâpâwêhisocik: they drowned themselves.

ê-kwêskîmot: he changes shape.

ê-mamâhtâwisit: he is spiritually powerful.

ê-mâyahkamikahk: where it went wrong, the Northwest Resistance of 1885.

ê-mistâpâwêhisocik: they drown themselves.

ê-pê-wîhtamân ê-maskawisît manitow: I come to tell that God is strong.

ê-sôhkêpayik: it is powerful.

ê-wî-nôtinitocik: they will fight each other.

ê-wî-pakwâtitocik: they will hate each other.

ê-wî-pôni-askîwik: the world will end.

hay! hay! thank you.

iskonikan: reserve; literally, "left-over."

iskotêw: the original "Burns," great-grandfather of Charlie Burns from James Smith reserve; literally, "fire."

ispîhk ê-kî-akohkasikêcik: when they were welding.

kawâhkatos: literally, "lean one"; Cree chief from the Treaty 4 area.

kâ-kisîwêw: Loud Voice; Cree chief.

kâ-kî-itiht: one who was called; said when naming someone deceased.

kâ-mâyahkamikahk: where it went wrong, the Northwest Resistance of 1885.

kâ-miyêstawêsit: Beardy; Cree chief.

kâ-miyikowisiyahk: what the Powers have given us (inclusive: all of us as Cree people).

kâ-miyikowisiyâhk: what the Powers have given us (exclusive: Cree people, not the addressee[s]).

kâ-papâmahcahkwêw: Wandering Spirit, leader of the *okihcitâwak*.

kâ-pitihkonâhk: Thunderchild reserve; named for the people of Sounding Lake (*nipiy kâ-pitihkwêk*).

kâ-têpwêwi-sîpiy: Qu'Appelle River; literally, "calling river."

kâ-wî-nânapâcihikoyâhk: that which is going to heal us.

kâkikê ka-pimi-tipahamâtân: I will forever make continuous payments to you for it.

kêhkêhk-iskwêw: Hawk Woman, Betsy McLeod; the wife of *nîkân-isi*. She was born around Shoal Lake; she died in 1957.

kêhtê-ayak: elders, old ones.

kêkâc: almost.

kihc-âtâwêwikamikwa: trading posts.

kihci- great.

kihci-manitow: the Creator, God.

kihci-okimâskwêw: queen; an older woman rich with relatives.

kimosômipaninawak: our (deceased) grandfathers.

kinosêw (fish), *otay* (Jackfish in Dene): one of the major signers of Treaty 8.

kistapinânihk: Prince Albert; literally, "the great or rich dwelling place."

kistêsinaw: our Elder Brother.

kiyâm: never mind; let it go.

kî-sâh-sîhcisiwak: they sat crowded together.

kotâwîwak: they enter into the ground.

kôkôcîs: Peter Vandall, my grandfather.

kwêcic: my grandmother from the Sandy Lake Reserve, a noted medicine woman.

mahkiyoc: literally, "the big one"; the everyday name of my ancestor, *nîkân-isi*, the original McLeod.

mamâhtâwi-âpacihcikan: computer; literally, "the machine which taps into the mystery of life."

mamâhtâwisiwin: tapping into the mystery.

manitow sâkahikan: God's Lake; a sacred site for both Cree and Saulteaux people, near what is today Watrous, Sask.; also the name of a lake near Neilburg, Sask.

manitowêw: Almighty Voice.

masaskêpiw: older brother of Chief *atâhkakohp*; my grandfather.

maskawisîw: he is strong.

mâmawi-ôhtâwîmâw: the All-Father, God.

mêmêkwêsiw: one of the Little People.

mêmêkwêsiwak: the Little People.

mêskanaw: road, trail; Meskanaw, Sask.

mihkomin sâkahikan: Redberry Lake.

minahikosis: Little Pine; Cree chief.

mistahi-maskwa: Big Bear; important Cree leader of the 1870s and 1880s.

mistanaskowêw: Calling Badger.

mistasiniy, mistasiniyak: grandfather stone(s); literally, "big stone(s)."

mistatim-awâsis: Horse Child, Big Bear's son.

mistawâsis: Big Child; Cree chief.

miyo-wîcihitowin: helping each other in a good way.

mosôm: grandfather; also vocative or address form (i.e., "Grandfather!").

môniyâw mistahi ê-iyinîsit: the white man is very intelligent.

môy ê-kistawêt: it doesn't echo (in reference to the land).

nayahcikan: bundle; literally, "something that you carry on your back."

nêhiyaw: Cree person.

nêhiyawak: Cree people.

nêhiyawaskiy: Cree territory.

nêhiyawêwin: Cree language.

nêhiyawi-itâpisiniwin: Cree worldview; literally, "a Cree viewpoint."

nêhiyâwiwin: Cree-ness.

nicâpân: my great-grandparent; my great-grandfather, Peter Vandall; my great-grandfather, Abel McLeod; my great-grandmother's sister, Betsy Head.

nihtâwikihcikanisihk: James Smith Reserve; literally, "the good growing place."

nikisêyinîwikwêmês: name of Old Man Buffalo in the story of Buffalo Child; literally, "my old man namesake."

nimosôm: my grandfather.

nipiy kâ-pitihkwêk: the term refers to Sounding Lake; literally, "rumbling water."

nîkân-isi: Thunderbird; literally, "the foremost one"; the name of my ancestor, the original McLeod.

nôhkom, nôhkomak: my grandmother(s).

nôtokwêw âtayôhkan: Grandmother Spirit.

okihcitâw, okihcitâwak: warrior(s), worthy young man (men).

okimâw: chief; someone with authority.

omitêw: a powerful person.

osâm iyinîsiw: he is too intelligent.

osâwâw-askiy-akohp: Yellow Mud Blanket; older brother of Chief *pîhtokahânapiwiyin* (Poundmaker); grandfather of John Tootoosis.

oskana kâ-asastêki: Regina, Sask.; literally, "Pile of Bones."

oskâpêwis: elder's helper or apprentice.

ôtê nîkân: the future; in the future.

paskwâ: literally, "prairie"; Cree chief Pasqua.

paskwâw-mostos awâsis: Buffalo Child.

pawâkan, pawâkanak: dream helper(s).

payipwât: Chief Piapot; chief of the *nêhiyawi-pwâtak* or Cree-Assiniboine band.

pâcinîs: Patrick Vandall; father of *kôkôcîs*, Peter Vandall.

pâstâhowin: transgression; bad karma.

pê-nânapâcihinân: come heal us.

pê-nîhtaciwêk: climb down.

pêhonânihk: Fort Carlton; literally, "the waiting place."

piyêsiw-awâsis: Thunderchild; Cree chief.

pîhtokahânapiwiyin: Poundmaker, Cree-Assiniboine leader.

pîkahin okosisa: the son of *pîkahin*. "*pîkahin*" is derived from the verb stem which means "to stir a liquid."

sasâkisîwak: Germans; literally, "they are selfish," in reference to the quest for land and empire in World War I.

sôhkêmakahk: it is powerful.

sôkâw-ministik: literally, "Sugar Island."

tapasî: run away.

tânisi ê-wî-ispayik: what is going to happen.

tipahamâtowin: Treaty; literally, "payment."

wâhkôhtowin: kinship.

wâskahikanis: Fort Pitt; literally, "small fort, small house."

wêpinâson: ceremonial cloth used as an offering.

wî-âyimahk: it is going to be difficult.

wîhcikôs: literally, "little *wîhtikow*"; endearing form of *wîhtikôhkân*.

wîhkasko-kisêyin: Old Man Sweetgrass; Cree chief.

wîhtikôhkân: my great-grandfather Peter Vandall's grandfather, a Dene from the Cold Lake area of Alberta; his brothers were *kinosêw* and *mostos*.

wîsahkêcâhk: the Cree transformer.

yêkawiskâwikamâhk: Sandy Lake, Ahtahkakoop (*atâhkakohp*) reserve.

NEAL MCLEOD'S FAMILY TREE

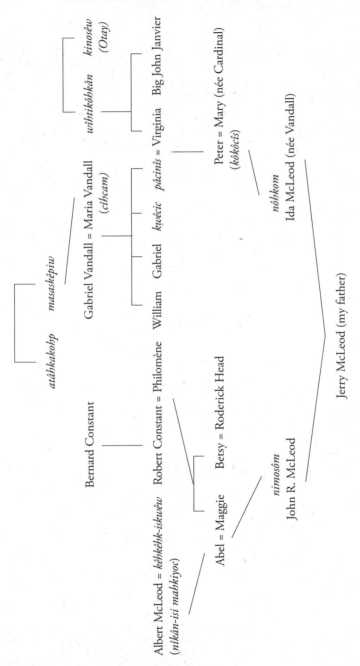

MAP OF LOCAL CREE TERRITORY

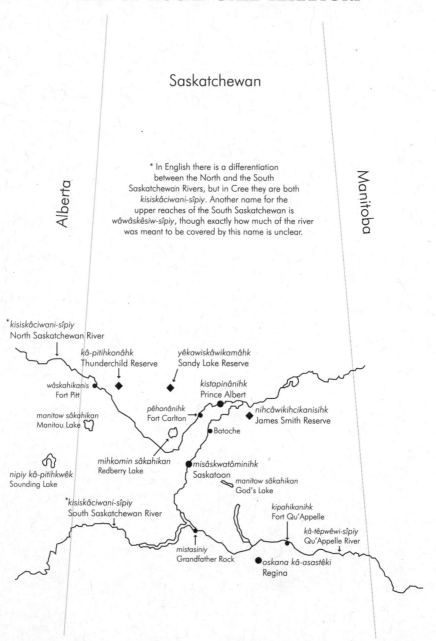

Saskatchewan

Alberta

Manitoba

* In English there is a differentiation between the North and the South Saskatchewan Rivers, but in Cree they are both *kisiskâciwani-sîpiy*. Another name for the upper reaches of the South Saskatchewan is *wâwâskêsiw-sîpiy*, though exactly how much of the river was meant to be covered by this name is unclear.

kisiskâciwani-sîpiy
North Saskatchewan River

kâ-pitihkonâhk
Thunderchild Reserve

yêkawiskâwikamâhk
Sandy Lake Reserve

wâskahikanis
Fort Pitt

kistapinânihk
Prince Albert

pêhonânihk
Fort Carlton

nihcâwikihcikanisihk
James Smith Reserve

manitow sâkahikan
Manitou Lake

Batoche

mihkomin sâkahikan
Redberry Lake

misâskwatôminihk
Saskatoon

manitow sâkahikan
God's Lake

nipiy kâ-pitihkwêk
Sounding Lake

kipahikanihk
Fort Qu'Appelle

kisiskâciwani-sîpiy
South Saskatchewan River

kâ-têpwêwi-sîpiy
Qu'Appelle River

mistasiniy
Grandfather Rock

oskana kâ-asastêki
Regina

Notes

Notes to Introduction

1 Vine Deloria, Jr., *God is Red: A Native View of Religion*, pp. 62-77.

2 Jim Kâ-Nîpitêhtêw, *kâtâayuk: Saskatchewan Indian Elders*. (Author's standard spelling would be *kêhtê-ayak*.)

3 Louise Bernice Halfe, *Blue Marrow*, p. 1.

4 *Ibid.*

5 *Ibid.*, p. 7.

6 *Ibid.*, p. 9.

7 Winona Stevenson, *Decolonizing Tribal Histories*, p. 79.

8 Halfe, p. 17.

9 *Ibid.*, p. 27.

10 Eli Bear, "Cree/Assiniboine Elders' Workshop," Jan. 29, 1974.

Notes to Chapter One

1 Keith Basso. *Wisdom Sits in Places: Landscape and Language Among the Western Apache*, p. 6.

2 Phillip Deloria, "Historiography," p. 16.

3 Richard Preston. *Cree Narratives: Expressing the Personal Meaning of Events*, p. 3.

4 Noel Dyck, "Negotiating the Indian 'Problem'," p. 132.

5 *Ibid.*, p. 136.

6 *Ibid.*, p. 138.

7 *Ibid.*

8 Robert Regnier, "John McLeod: First Nations Educator."

9 Freda Ahenakew and H. C. Wolfart (Eds. and Trans.), *ana kâ-pimwêwêhahk okakêskihkêmowina / The Counselling Speeches of Jim Kâ-Nîpitêhtêw.*

10 *Ibid.*, p. 106.

11 *Ibid.*, p. 106.

12 Walter Lightning, "Compassionate Mind: Implications of a text written by Elder Louis Sunchild," p. 216.

13 *Ibid.*

14 Linda Tuhiwai Smith, *Decolonizing Methodologies*, p. 31.

15 David Meyer, *The Red Earth Crees*, 1860-1960, p. 52.

NOTES TO CHAPTER TWO

1   Isadore Pelletier, interview, Dec. 14, 2004.

2   *Ibid.*, p. 2.

3   *Ibid.*

4   Stan Cuthand, "*mistasiniy,*" p. 31.

5   Henry Cardinal, interview, p. 10.

6   *Ibid.*, p. 9.

7   Cuthand, "*mistasiniy,*" pp. 31-32.

8   Thanks to Jean Okimâsis and Arok Wolvengrey for helping decipher this name from the transcript.

9   Cuthand, "*mistasiniy,*" p. 34.

10 Gabriel Crow Buffalo, presentation to Cree History and Culture Class, Nov. 23, 2003.

11 Alexander Wolfe, *Earth Elder Stories*, pp. 5-9.

12 Cuthand, "*mistasiniy,*" pp. 30-34.

13 Barry Ahenakew, "*mostos-awâsis*" [Buffalo Boy], pp. 25-46.

14 *Ibid.*, p. 39.

15 *Ibid.*, p. 45.

16 *Ibid.*

17 Cardinal, interview.

18 *Ibid.*, p. 10.

19 Pelletier, interview, p. 3.

20 "Thunderbirds," produced by Maureen Matthews. *Ideas*, CBC Radio, May 15, 16, 1995.

21 David Laird to Lawrence Vankoughnet, Nov. 12, 1878.

22 Clifford Sanderson, personal communication, Aug. 17, 2003.

23 Charlie Burns, interview, Feb. 15, 2003.

24 *Ibid.*

25 Jerry McLeod, interview, June 25, 2000.

26 Josie Whitehead and Helen Whitehead, conversation, 1976.

27 Robert Brightman, *âcathôhkîwina and âcimôwina*.

28 Sanderson, personal communication.

29 Barry Ahenakew, 2000, pp. 62-81.

30 *Ibid.*, p. 65.

31 Robert Brightman, *Grateful Prey: Rock Cree Human-Animal Relationships*, p. 87.

32 *Ibid.*, p. 87.

33 Willie Ermine, "Aboriginal Epistemology," pp. 101-112.

34 Sanderson, personal communication.

35 Sarah Whitecalf, *kinêhiyâwiwininaw nêhiyawêwin / The Cree language Is Our Identity: The La Ronge Lectures of Sarah Whitecalf, p. 37.*

36 Ermine, "Aboriginal Epistemology," p. 35.

37 Norval Morrisseau, *Travels to the House of Invention.*

38 *Ibid.*, p. 13.

39 *Ibid.*, p. 22.

40 Brightman, *Grateful Prey*, p. 81.

41 Morrisseau, *Travels to the House of Invention*, p. 15.

42 Peter Vandall, *wâskahikaniwiyiniw-âcimowina / Stories of the House People*, pp. 48-49.

43 Eli Bear, "Cree/Assiniboine Elders' Workshop," p. 9.

Notes to Chapter Three

1   John R. McLeod, "Address by John McLeod to Treaty #6 Commemoration," p. 1.

2   *Ibid.*, p. 2.

3   Sharon Venne, "Understanding Treaty 6: An Indigenous Perspective," p. 181.

4   Julian Moses, minutes from Treaty 6 Commemoration Meeting, p. 8.

5   National Archives of Canada (NAC), RG 10, Vol. 1847, File IT 296/157A.

6   J. E. Foster, "Indian-White Relations in the Prairie West During the Fur Trade Period — A Compact?" p. 195.

7   John Milloy, *A National Crime: The Canadian Government and the Residential School System, 1879-1986*, p. 107.

8   Arthur Ray, J. R. Miller, and Frank Tough, *Bounty and Benevolence: A Documentary History of Saskatchewan Treaties*, p. 146.

9   Foster, "Indian-White Relations," p. 200.

10 John Leonard Taylor, "Canada's Northwest Indian Policy in the 1870s: Traditional Premises and Necessary Innovations," p. 40.

11 International Work Group for Indigenous Affairs (IWGIA), *Honour Bound: Onion Lake and the Spirit of Treaty 6*, IWGIA Document No 84. (Copenhagen, 1997); see also various interviews from the Indian History Film Project.

12 Alexander Morris, *The Treaties of Canada with the Indians of Manitoba and the North-West Territories*, p. 74.

13 *Ibid.*, p. 174.

14 *Ibid.*

15   Laura Peers, *The Ojibwa of Western Canada: 1780 to 1870.*

16   François Dufresne, "Defense of Big Bear," pp. 6-7.

17   Morris, *The Treaties of Canada*, p. 175.

18   *Ibid.*, p. 191.

19   W. B. Fraser, "Big Bear: Indian Patriot," p. 4.

20   Ray et al.

21   *Ibid.*, p. 141.

22   Morris, *The Treaties of Canada*, p. 191.

23   Coming Day, "Sweetgrass Defeats the Blackfoot and Sarci,", p. 37.

24   Morris, *The Treaties of Canada*, p. 240.

25   Alex Stick, interview, Feb. 18, 1974, p. 2.

26   *Ibid.*

27   *Ibid.*

28   John L. Tobias, "Canada's Subjugation of the Plains Cree, 1879-1885," p. 523.

29   D. J. Hall, "'A Serene Atmosphere'? Treaty 1 Revisited," p. 322.

30   *Ibid.*, p. 324.

31   Alexander Morris, Letter to the Minister of the Interior, March 2, 1877.

32   *Ibid.*

33   *Ibid.*

34   Robert Smallboy, interview, n.d., p. 2.

35   IWGIA, *Honour Bound*, p. 67.

36   *Ibid.*, p. 61.

37   *Ibid.*, p. 72.

38   Smallboy, interview, n.d., p. 3.

39   *Ibid.*

Notes to Chapter Four

1   National Archives of Canada (NAC), RG 10, Vol. 3670, File 10771.

2   *Ibid.*

3   *Ibid.*

4   *Ibid.*

5   *Ibid.*

6   International Work Group for Indigenous Affairs (IWGIA), *Honour Bound*, p. 76.

7   Edward Ahenakew, *Voices of the Plains Cree*, p. 11.

8   Freda Ahenakew and H. C. Wolfart (Eds. and Trans.), *ana kâ-pimwêwêhahk okakêskihkêmowina / The Counselling Speeches of Jim Kâ-Nîpitêhtêw*, p. 111.

9   *Ibid.*

10   John Buffalo, interview, 1975, p. 6.

11   Lazarus Roan, interview, 1974, pp. 2-3.

12   James Bull, interview, 1973, p. 3.

13   W. B. Fraser, "Big Bear: Indian Patriot," p. 8.

14   NAC, RG 10, Vol. 3576, File 309 A.

15   *Ibid.*

16   Rae to Dewdney, *Ibid.*

17   NAC, RG 10, Vol. 3576, File 309 A.

18   *Ibid.*

19   *Ibid.*

20   *Ibid.*

21   *Ibid.*

22   *Ibid.*

23   Hugh Dempsey, *Big Bear and the End of Freedom*, p. 142.

24   *Queen* vs. *Big Bear*, Sessional Papers, 1886, No. 52., p. 182.

25   Dempsey, *Big Bear and the End of Freedom*, p. 117.

26   Desmond Morton and Reginald H. Roy, *Telegrams of the North-west Campaign, 1885*, pp. 161, 317-318.

27   *Queen* vs. *Big Bear*, p. 206.

28   François Dufresne, "Defense of Big Bear," p. 6.

29   *Queen* vs. *Big Bear*, p. 177.

30   *Ibid.*, p. 189.

31   *Ibid.*, p. 190.

32   *Ibid.*

33   *Ibid.*

34   NAC, RG 10, Vol. 3774, File 36846.

35   *Ibid.*

36   *Ibid.*

37   NAC, RG 10, Vol. 3576, File 309 A, Document 97.

38   Royal Commission on Aboriginal Peoples, "Vol. II. Restructuring the Relationship," p. 37.

39   Dufresne, "Defense of Big Bear," p. 7.

NOTES TO CHAPTER FIVE

1   Edward Ahenakew, *Voices of the Plains Cree*, p. 71.

2   *Ibid.*, p. 72.

3   Jeanettte C. Armstrong, "The Disempowerment of First North American Native Peoples and Empowerment Through Their Writing," p. 239.

4   Robert Regnier, "John McLeod: First Nations Educator," p. 4.

5   *Ibid.*, p. 6.

6   Quoted in Donna Philips, Robert Troff, and Harvery Whitecalf, *kâhtâayuk: Saskatchewan Indian Elders*, n.p.

7   Norma Sluman and Jean Goodwill, *John Tootoosis*, p. 106.

8   *kâhtâayuk: Saskatchewan Indian Elders*, n.p.

9   *Ibid.*

NOTES TO CHAPTER SIX

1   "Saulteaux Elders Workshop #1," 1973.

2   The preceding narrative is from Jerry McLeod, interview, June 25, 2000.

3   Maureen Lux, *Medicine that Walks: Disease, Medicine and Canadian Plains Native People, 1880-1940*, pp. 4, 10.

4   Edward Ahenakew, *Voices of the Plains Cree*, p. xii.

5   *Ibid.*, p. 62.

6   Peter Vandall, *wâskahikaniwiyiniw-âcimowina*, pp. 65-69.

7   *Ibid.*, p. 65.

8   *Ibid.*, pp. 64-69.

9   *Proceedings of the Plains Cree Conference* held in Fort Qu'Appelle, Sask., p. 23.

10   Gerald Vizenor, *Wordarrows: Indians and Whites in the New Fur Trade.*

11   Ahenakew, *Voices of the Plains Cree*, p. 51.

12   John R. McLeod, "In the Spirit of Our Forefathers," videotape, 1981.

13   Keith Basso, *Wisdom Sits in Places.*

14   Julie Cruikshank, *Life Lived like a Story: Life Stories of Three Yukon Elders.*

15   David Newhouse, *From the Tribal to the Modern: The Development of Modern Societies.*

NOTES TO CHAPTER SEVEN

1   David Meyer, *The Red Earth Crees*, pp. 278-279.

2   Charlie Burns, interview, Feb. 15, 2003.

3   *Ibid.*

4   Betsy Head, interview, May 1998.

5   Burns, interview, 2003.

6   *Ibid.*

7   Clifford Sanderson, personal communication, Aug. 17, 2003.

8   Charlie Burns, interview, July 24, 2004(a).

9   Bill Stonestand, tape recording, Nov. 5, 1995.

10 Bill Stonestand, interview, Nov. 1996.

11 Burns, interview, 2004(a).

12 Burns, interview, 2003.

13 Stonestand, tape recording, 1995.

14 *Ibid.*

15 *Ibid.*

16 Charlie Burns, interview, Sep. 11, 2004(b).

17 *Ibid.*

18 Burns, 2003.

19 Jerry McLeod. Interview with author, James Smith Reserve, June 25, 2000.

20 Burns, 2003.

21 Burns, 2004(b).

22 Burns, 2004(a).

23 *Ibid.*

24 Stonestand, 1995, 1996.

25 Stonestand, 1995.

26 *Ibid.*

NOTES TO CHAPTER EIGHT

1   Jerry McLeod, interview, June 25, 2000.

2   *Ibid.*

3   Burton Vandall, interview, April 17, 2005.

4   John R. McLeod, "Addresss by John McLeod to Treaty #6 Commemoration,"
    1975(b), p. 2.

5   See J. E. Foster, "Indian-White Relations in the Prairie West during the Fur Trade Period — A Compact?" pp. 181-200.

6   John Tootoosis, *Towards a New Past*, interview, Sept. 9, 1977.

7   Federation of Saskatchewan Indians, Constitutional Position on the Entrenchment of Aboriginal and Treaty Rights (Draft), Sept. 1980.

8   John Tootoosis, *Towards a New Past.*

9   *Ibid.*

10 *Ibid.*

11 *Ibid.*

12 Norma Sluman and Jean Goodwill, *John Tootoosis*, p. 107.

13 Wilfred Tootoosis, interview, *Words of Elders: Aboriginal Cultures in Transition*, p. 314.

14 Pat Cayen, personal communication, 1999.

15 Union of Saskatchewan Indians, *Constitution and Minutes of Meeting*, 1946, p. 1.

16 *Ibid.*, p. 5.

17 Sixth Annual School Committee Conference, May 1-2, p. 4.

18 Blue Quills Native Education Council, untitled document, 1970.

19 National Indian Brotherhood, Indian Control of Indian Education, p. 9.

20 *Ibid.*, p. 2.

21 Jean Barman, Yvonne Hébert, and Don McCaskill, "The Challenge of Indian Education: An Overview," p. 21.

22 Saskatchewan Indian Cultural College, Proposal for a New School to Serve Little Pine, Lucky Man, Poundmaker, p. 8.

23 Barman, Hébert, and McCaskill, p. 2.

24 *Ibid.*, p. 1.

25 "The Louse that Roared," *Saskatchewan Indian,* Jan. 1974, p. 26.

26 Noel Dyck and John R. McLeod, "Report on the Recent Events of the Removal of the Students from Kinistino Schools and the Expansion of the James Smith Schools," May 1973, p. 1.

27 Conversation with the author, n.d.

28 John L. Tobias to John R. McLeod, May 2, 1973.

29 John R. McLeod, 1975b, p. 14.

30 *Ibid.*, p. 14.

31 John R. McLeod, "Treaty 6 Commemoration Meeting," Jan. 19-20, 1976, p. 6.

32 John R. McLeod, 1975b, p. 2.

33 *Ibid.*, p. 3.

NOTES TO CHAPTER NINE

1   John R. McLeod, minutes from Treaty 6 General Meeting, 1975a, p. 6.

2   N. Scott Momaday, *The Man Made of Words*, p. 7.

3   *Ibid.*, p. 8.

4   Harry Blackbird, http://www.horizonzero.ca/elderspeak/stories/creeway.html.

5   Maria Campbell, *Halfbreed*, p. 86.

6   Edward Ahenakew, *Voices of the Plains Cree*, p. 52.

7   *Ibid.*, p. 62.

8   *Ibid.*, p. 51.

9   Jim Kâ-Nîpitêhtêw, *The Counselling Speeches of Jim Kâ-Nîpitêhtêw*.

10 Gerald Vizenor, *Wordarrows: Indians and Whites in the New Fur Trade*.

11 Martin Heidegger, "The Question Concerning Technology," in *Martin Heidegger: Basic Writings*, 1977.

12 Mikhail Bakhtin, *The Dialogic Imagination: Four Essays*, p. 426.

Selected Bibliography

Ahenakew, Barry. "*mostos-awâsis*" [Buffalo Boy] in *Ahtahkakoop: The Epic Account of a Plains Cree Head Chief, His Peoples, and Their Vision For Survival, 1816-1896.* Edited by Deanna Christensen (Shell Lake, Sask.: Ahtahkakoop Nation, 2000).

Ahenakew, Edward. *Voices of the Plains Cree.* Edited by Ruth Buck; foreword by Stan Cuthand. (Regina: Canadian Plains Research Centre, 1995).

Ahenakew, Freda (Ed. and Trans.), *kiskinahamawâkan-âcimowinisa: Student Stories* (Saskatoon: Saskatchewan Indian Cultural Centre, 1989).

_____ (Ed. and Trans.), *wâskahikaniwiyiniw-âcimowina: Stories of the House People. Cree Texts of Peter Vandall and Joe Duquette* (Winnipeg: University of Manitoba Press, 1987).

_____ (Ed. and Trans.). *kôhkominawak otâcimowiniwâwa: Our Grandmothers' Lives as Told in Their Own Words* (Regina: Canadian Plains Research Centre, 1998).

_____ (Ed. and Trans.). *kwayask ê-kî-pê-kiskinowâpahtihicik: Their Example Showed Me the Way: Cree texts of Ema Minde* (Edmonton: University of Alberta Press, 1997).

_____ (Ed. and Trans.) *kinêhiyâwiwininaw nêhiyawêwin: The Cree Language is Our Identity. Cree texts of Sarah Whitecalf* (Winnipeg: University of Manitoba Press, 1993).

Ahenakew, Freda and H. C. Wolfart, (Eds. & Trans.), *âh-âyîtaw isi ê-kî-kiskêyihtahkik maskihkiy / They Knew Both Sides of Medicine: Cree Tales of Curing and Cursing Told by Alice Ahenakew* (Winnipeg: University of Manitoba Press, 2000).

_____ (Eds. & Trans.). *ana kâ-pimwêwêhahk okakêskihkêmowina / The Counselling Speeches of Jim Kâ-Nîpitêhtêw* (Winnipeg: University of Manitoba Press, 1998).

Alfred, Gerald. *Heeding the Voices of our Ancestors* (Toronto: Oxford University Press, 1995).

Alfred, Taiaiake. *Peace, Power, Righteousness: An Indigenous Manifesto* (Toronto: Oxford University Press, 1999).

Allen, R.S. "Big Bear," *Saskatchewan History* 25, 1 (1972): 1-17.

Anon. "Saulteaux Elders Workshop #1," IH-427, Sept. Speakers are unidentified. Indian History Film Project, SIFC (SIFC) Library, Office of Specific Claims and Research, 1973.

Armstrong, Jeanette C. "The Disempowerment of First North American Native Peoples and Empowerment through Their Writing," in *An Anthology of Canadian Native Literature in English,* 2nd edition. Edited by Daniel David Moses and Terry Goldie (Toronto: Oxford University Press, 1998), pp. 239-242.

Asapace, Sarah. *Enewuk* (Saskatoon: Saskatchewan Indian Cultural College, 1978).

Atimoyoo, Smith. *The Saskatchewan Indian Cultural College*. Film. (Saskatoon: SIFC, 1975).

Bakhtin, Mikhail. *The Dialogic Imagination: Four Essays*. Edited by Michael Holquist. Translated by Caryl Emerson and Michael Holquist (Austin: University of Texas Press, 1981).

Barman, Jean, Yvonne Hébert, and Don McCaskill. "The Challenge of Indian Education: An Overview" in *Indian Education in Canada*, Vol. 2: *The Challenge* (Vancouver: UBC Press, 1999), pp. 1-21.

Basso, Keith. *Wisdom Sits in Places: Landscape and Language Among the Western Apache* (Albuquerque: University of New Mexico Press, 1996).

_____. *Portraits of "The Whiteman": Linguistic Play and Cultural Symbols among the Western Apache* (New York: Cambridge University Press, 1979).

Bear, Eli. "Cree / Assiniboine Elders' Workshop," Saskatchewan Indian Cultural Centre, Jan. 29, 1974. SIFC Library, IH-434.

Bear, Robert. Quoted in *kâhtâayuk: Saskatchewan Indian Elders*. Edited by Donna Philips, Robert Troff, and Harvery Whitecalf (Saskatoon: Saskatchewan Indian Cultural College, 1976), n.p.

Bloomfield, Leonard. *Plains Cree Texts* (New York: G. E. Stechert, 1934).

Blue Quills Native Education Council. Untitled document from the private papers of John R. McLeod, 1970.

Brightman, Robert. *Grateful Prey: Rock Cree Human-Animal Relationships* (Berkeley: University of California Press, 1993).

_____. *âcathôhkîwina and âcimôwina* (Ottawa: National Museum of Civilization, 1989).

Buffalo, John. Interview with Richard Lightning in *Spirit and Terms of Treaty 6, 7 & 8* (Edmonton: Indian Association of Alberta, 1975).

Bull, James. Interview with Abraham Burnstick. Indian History Film Project, SIFC Library, Office of Specific Claims and Research, 1973. IH-171.

Burns, Charlie. Interview with author. July 24, 2004(a). Prince Albert, Sask. (at his home).

_____. Interview with author. Sept. 11, 2004(b). Prince Albert.

_____. Interview with author. Feb. 15, 2003. Duck Lake, Sask..

Campbell, Maria. *Halfbreed* (Toronto: McClelland and Stewart, 1973).

Cameron, William. *Blood Red the Sun* (Calgary: Kenway, 1950).

Canadian Plains Research Centre. Proceedings of the Plains Cree Conference held in Fort Qu'Appelle, Sask. (Regina: Canadian Plains Research Centre, Oct. 24-26, 1975).

Cardinal, Henry. Interview with Richard Lightning in *Saddle Lake Interviews*. Indian History Film Project, SIFC Library, Office of Specific Claims and Research, 1975. IH-220.

Carter, Sarah. *Lost Harvests: Prairie Indian Reserve Farmers and Government Policy* (Montreal and Kingston: McGill-Queen's University Press, 1993).

Cavender Wilson, Angela. "Grandmother to Granddaughter: Generations of Oral History in a Dakota Family," in *Natives and Academics: Researching and Writing about American Indians*. Edited by Devon Mihesuah (Lincoln: University of Nebraska Press, 1998), pp. 27-36.

Cayen, Pat. Personal communication, 1999.

Chief, Charlie. Interview with Alphonse Littlepoplar, Seekaskootch Reserve, July 11, 1974. Indian History Film Project, SIFC Library, Saskatchewan Archives Board, 1974. IH-029 / 30.

Chief, Jimmy. Interview with Mary Mountain, Seekaskootch Reserve, July 23, 1973. Indian History Film Project, Saskatchewan Archives Board, 1973. IH-026.

Christensen, Deanna. *Ahtahkakoop* (Shell Lake, Sask.: Ahtahkakoop Publishing, 2000).

Coleman, Michael. "The Responses of American Indian Children and Irish Children to the School, 1850s-1920s: A Comparative Study in Cross-Cultural Education," in *American Indian Quarterly* 23, 3 & 4 (1999): 83-112.

Coming Day. "Sweetgrass Defeats the Blackfoot and Sarci," in *Plains Cree Texts*. Collected by Leonard Bloomfield (New York: G. E. Stechert and Company, 1934), pp. 35-41.

Crow Buffalo, Gabriel. Presentation to Cree History and Culture Class. First Nations University of Canada, field trip to Fort Qu'Appelle, Nov. 23, 2003.

Cruikshank, Julie. *Life Lived like a Story: Life Stories of Three Yukon Elders* (Vancouver: UBC Press, 1990).

Cuthand, Stan. "*mistasiniy*," in *Native Religious Traditions*. Edited by Earle H. Waugh, and K. Dad Prithipaul (Waterloo, Ont: Wilfrid Laurier University Press, 1979), pp. 31-34.

Darnell, Regna. "The Implications of Cree Interactional Etiquette," in *Native North American Interaction Patterns*. Edited by Regna Darnell and Michael K. Foster (Ottawa: Canadian Museum of Civilization, National Museums of Canada, 1988), pp. 69-77.

Deloria, Phillip. "Historiography," in *A Companion to American Indian History*. Edited by Phillip J. Deloria and Neal Salisbury (Malden, Mass.: Blackwell, 2002).

Deloria Jr., Vine. *Custer Died for Your Sins* (Norman: University of Oklahoma Press, 1988 / 1969).

_____. *For this Land: Writings on Religion in America* (New York: Routledge, 1999).

_____. *God is Red: A Native View of Religion* (Golden, Colo.: Fulcrum, 1994 / 1972).

Demallie, Raymond J. "The Lakota Ghost Dance: An Ethnohistorical Account," *Pacific Historical Review*, 51, 2 (1982): 385-405.

Dempsey, Hugh. *Big Bear and the End of Freedom* (Lincoln: University of Nebraska Press, 1984).

Dufresne, François. "Defense of Big Bear." Supplement to *The Western Producer*, June 16 (1983): 10-11. Interviewer: Humphrey Gratz. Onion Lake Reserve. Reprinted from *Western People*, 1941.

Dyck, Noel. "Negotiating the Indian 'Problem'," in *The First Ones: Readings in Indian / Native Studies*. Edited by David Miller et al,. (Piapot Reserve: SIFC Press, 1992), pp. 132-140.

_____. *What is the Indian "Problem"? Tutelage and Resistance in Canadian Indian Administration* (St. John's, Nfld: Memorial University of Newfoundland, 1991).

Dyck, Noel and John R. McLeod. "Report on the Recent Events of the Removal of the Students from Kinistino Schools and the Expansion of the James Smith Schools" (May 1973).

Eakin, Paul. *How our Lives Become Stories* (Ithaca, NY: Cornell University Press, 1999).

Erasmus, Peter. *Buffalo Days and Nights.* Translated by Henry Thompson (Calgary: Fifth House, 1999).

Ermine, Willie. (1998). "Pedagogy from the Ethos: An Interview with Elder Ermine on Language," in *As We See . . . Aboriginal Pedagogy.* Edited by Lenore Stiffarm (Saskatoon: University of Saskatchewan Extension Press, 1998), pp. 9-28.

_____. "Aboriginal Epistemology," in *First Nations Education in Canada: The Circle Unfolds.* Edited by Marie Battiste and Jean Barman (Vancouver: UBC Press, 1995), pp. 101-112.

Fanon, Frantz. *The Wretched of the Earth.* Translated by Constance Farrington (New York: Grove Press, 1963).

Federation of Saskatchewan Indians. Constitutional Position on the Entrenchment of Aboriginal and Treaty Rights (Draft). Prepared by Delia Opekokew (Sept. 1980).

Fenton, William N. *The Great Law and the Longhouse: A Political History of the Iroquois Confederacy* (Norman: University of Oklahoma Press, 1998).

_____. *American Indian and White Relations to 1830: Needs and Opportunities for Study* (Chapel Hill: University of North Carolina Press, 1957).

Fine Day. Interview with Dr. D. G. Mandelbaum, Sweet Grass Reserve, Sept. 10, 1934. Indian History Film Project, SIFC Library, Dr. D. G. Mandelbaum, IH-DM.61.

Fitzpatrick, David. "Flight from Famine," in *The Great Irish Famine*. Edited by Cathal Póirtéir (Chester Springs, Penn.: Dufour Editions, 1995), pp. 174-184.

Flanagan, Thomas. *First Nations? Second Thoughts* (Montreal and Kingston: McGill-Queen's University Press, 2000).

Foster, J. E. "Indian-White Relations in the Prairie West during the Fur Trade Period – A Compact?" in *The Spirit of Alberta Indian Treaties*. Edited by Richard Price (Edmonton: Pica Pica Press, 1987), pp. 181-200.

Fox, Edward. Minutes from Treaty 6 General Meeting, Beardy's Reserve, Nov. 27, 1975. Beardy's Band Hall. From the private papers of John R. McLeod.

Fraser, W. B. "Big Bear, Indian Patriot," *Alberta Historical Review* 14, 2 (1966): 1-13.

Frizzly Bear. Quoted in *kâhtâayuk: Saskatchewan Indian Elders*. Edited by Donna Philips, Robert Troff, and Harvery Whitecalf (Saskatoon: Saskatchewan Indian Cultural College, 1976), n.p.

Habermas, Jürgen. "Modernity versus Postmodernity." Translated by Seyla ben Habib. *New German Critique* 22 (1981): 3-14.

Haig-Brown, Celia and Kaaren Dannenmann. "A Pedagogy of the Land: Dreams of Respectful Relations," *Revue des Sciences de l'éducation de McGill* 37, 3 (2002): 451-468.

Halfe, Louise Bernice. *Blue Marrow* (Regina: Coteau Books, 2004).

Hall, D.J. "'A Serene Atmosphere'? Treaty 1 Revisted." *Canadian Journal of Native Studies* 4, 2 (1984): 321-358.

Harper, Francis Michael. "Married Couples Workshop 158 - #4," Nov. 15, 1973. CD 00347 (Saskatchewan Indian Cultural College, 1973).

Harris, Cole. "Power, Modernity and Historical Geography," *Annals of the Association of American Geographers,* 81, 4 (1991): 671-683.

Head, Betsy. Interview with author, James Smith Reserve, May 1998.

Heidegger, Martin. "The Question Concerning Technology," in *Basic Writings of Martin Heidegger*. Edited by David Krell (San Francisco: Harper & Row, 1977), pp. 283-317.

_____. *Being and Time*. Translated by John Macquarrie and Edward Robinson (New York: Harper and Row, 1967/1927).

Hodgson, Eugene. "Saskatchewan School Committee." Unpublished paper (Saskatoon, Sask., n.d.).

Horse, Fred. Interview with Louis Rain in *Spirit and Terms of Treaties 6, 7 & 8: Alberta Indian Perspectives*. Edited by Richard Price (Edmonton: Indian Association of Alberta, 1975).

_____. Interview with Louis Rain, Louis Bull Reserve, Alta., Feb. 18, 1974. Indian History Film Project, SIFC Library, Office of Specific Claims and Research. IH-186A.

_____. Interview with Louis Rain, Louis Bull Reserve, Alta., Feb. 18, 1974. Indian History Film Project, SIFC Library, Office of Specific Claims and Research. IH-187B.

Huggan, Graham. "Decolonizing the Map: Post-Colonialism, Post-Structuralism and the Cartographic Connection," *Ariel* 20 (4), 1989: 115-129.

Indian and Northern Affairs. James Smith Band Audit, 1973-1974. From the private papers of John R. McLeod.

International Work Group for Indigenous Affairs (IWGIA). *Honour Bound: Onion Lake and the Spirit of Treaty 6. The International Validity of Treaties with Indigenous People*. IWGIA Document No. 84 (Copenhagen: IWGIA, 1997).

Jacobs, Allen. Personal communication, 2000.

James Smith Land Register.

Johnston, Basil. "One Generation from Extinction," in *An Anthology of Canadian Native Literature in English*, 2nd ed. Edited by Daniel David Moses and Terry Goldie (Toronto: Oxford University Press, 1998), pp. 99-104.

Joseph, Mel. Counselling Speech at a Round Dance in Saskatoon, Sask., Nov. 22, 1997.

kâ-kîsikâw pîhtokêw (Coming Day). *Sacred Stories of the Sweet Grass Cree*. Edited and translated by Leonard Bloomfield (New York: AMS Press, 1930).

Kâ-Nîpitêhtêw, Jim. *ana kâ-pimwêwêhahk okakêskihkêmowina / The Counselling Speeches of Jim Kâ-Nîpitêhtêw*. Edited and translated by Freda Ahenakew and H. C. Wolfart (Winnipeg: University of Manitoba Press, 1998).

_____. Interview in *kâtâayuk: Saskatchewan Indian Elders* (Saskatchewan Indian Cultural College, 1976), n.p.

Krupat, Arnold. *The Turn to the Native: Studies in Criticism and Culture* (Lincoln: University of Nebraska Press, 1996).

Laroque, Emma. "On the Ethics of Publishing Historical Documents," in *"The Orders of the Dreamed": George Nelson on Cree and Northern Ojibwa Religion and Myth, 1823*. Edited by Jennifer S. H. Brown and Robert Brightman (Winnipeg: University of Manitoba Press, 1988), pp. 199-203.

Lavallee, Beatrice. Interview with author, Elders' Lounge, SIFC, July 2001.

Lightning, Walter. "Compassionate Mind: Implications of a Text Written by Elder Louis Sunchild," *Canadian Journal of Native Studies* (1992): 216.

Littlejohn, Catherine. *The Indian Oral Tradition: A Model for Teachers*. Master's thesis (Saskatoon: University of Saskatchewan, College of Education, 1975).

Lonethunder, Sandy. "Cree / Assiniboine Elder Workshop," Saskatchewan Indian Cultural College, Jan. 29, 1974. Indian History Film Project, SIFC Library. IH-432.

Longboat, Dianne. "First Nation Control of Education: The Path to Our Survival," in *Indian Education in Canada*. Vol. 2: *The Challenge*. Edited by Jean Barman, Yvonne Hébert, and Don McCaskill (Vancouver: UBC Press, 1999/1986), pp. 22-42.

Lux, Maureen. *Medicine that Walks: Disease, Medicine and Canadian Plains Native People, 1880-1940*. (Toronto: University of Toronto Press, 2001).

Mandelbaum, David. *The Plains Cree* (Regina: Canadian Plains Research Centre, 1994 / 1979).

_____. (Ed.). *Selected Writings of Edward Sapir* (Berkeley: University of California Press, 1958).

Marken, Ron. "'There is Nothing but White between the Lines': Parallel Colonial Experiences of the Irish and Aboriginal Canadians," in *Native North America: Critical and Cultural Perspectives*. Edited by Renée Hulan (Toronto: ECW Press, 1999), pp. 156-173.

McFarlene, Peter. *Brotherhood to Nationhood: George Manuel and the Making of the Modern Indian Movement* (Toronto: Between the Lines, 1993).

McLeod, Jerry. Conversation with author, James Smith Reserve, June 25, 2000.

McLeod, Jerry and Burton Vandall. Interview with author about Gabriel Vandall, World War II veteran, James Smith Reserve, April 17, 2005.

McLeod, John R. "Addresss by John McLeod to Treaty #6 Commemoration." Presented to the All Chiefs Conference, April 20, 1975. From the private papers of John R. McLeod, 1975(b).

_____. *In the Spirit of Our Forefathers*. Videotape (Saskatoon: SIFC, 1981).

_____. Minutes from Treaty 6 General Meeting, Onion Lake Band Hall, Onion Lake, Sask., Dec. 11, 1975. From the private papers of John R. McLeod, 1975(a).

_____. Treaty 6 Commemoration Meeting, Thunderchild Reserve, Jan. 19 - 20, 1976.

McLeod, Neal. *Songs to Kill a Wîhtikow* (Regina: Hagios Press, 2005).

Metchewais, Alexander. Interview with Richard Lightning in *Spirit and Terms of Treaty 6, 7 & 8*. Edited by Richard Price. Translated by Richard Lightning (Edmonton: Indian Association of Alberta, 1975).

Meyer, David. *The Red Earth Crees, 1860-1960* (Ottawa: National Museums of Canada, 1985).

Miller, J. R. *Shingwauk's Visions: Native Residential Schools in Canada* (Toronto: University of Toronto Press, 1996).

Miller, Melvin E. "Ethics and Understanding through Interrelationship: I and Thou in Dialogue," in *The Narrative Study of Lives*. Edited by Ruthellen Josselson (Thousand Oaks: Sage, 1996), pp. 45- 59.

Milloy, John. *"A National Crime": The Canadian Government and the Residential School System, 1879-1986* (Winnipeg: University of Manitoba Press, 1999).

_____. *The Plains Cree: Trade, Diplomacy and War, 1790 to 1870* (Winnipeg: University of Manitoba Press, 1990).

Momaday, N. Scott. *The Man Made of Words* (New York: St. Martin's Griffin, 1997).

Morris, Alexander. Letter to the Minister of the Interior, March 2, 1877. Alexander Morris Papers.

_____. *Treaties of Canada with the Indians of Manitoba and the North-West Territories* (Fifth House: Saskatoon, 1991/1880).

Morrisseau, Norval. *Travels to the House of Invention* (Toronto: Key Porter, 1997).

Morton, Desmond and Reginald H. Roy (Eds.). *Telegrams of the North-west Campaign, 1885* (Toronto: Champlain Society, 12972).

Moses, Julian. Minutes of Treaty 6 Commemoration Meeting, Onion Lake, Sask., Dec. 5, 1975. From the private papers of John R. McLeod.

Nabokov, Peter. *A Forest of Time: American Indian Ways of History* (New York: Cambridge University Press, 2002).

National Archives of Canada. Chiefs' Petition to Release Big Bear, Jan. 25, 1887. RG 10, Vol. 3774, File 36846.

_____. Edgar Dewdney, Feb. 12, 1885. RG 10, Vol. 3576, File 309 A.

_____. Francis J. Dickens to Edgar Dewdney. RG 10, Vol. 3576, File 309 A.

_____. David Laird to Lawrence Vankoughnet, Nov. 12, 1878. RG 10, Vol. 3670, File 10771.

_____. Memo of promises to Big Bear, June 12, 1883. RG 10, Vol. 3576, File 309 A.

_____. J. M. Rae to Edgar Dewdney, July 20, 1884. RG 10, Vol. 3576, File 309 A.

_____. J. M. Rae to Edgar Dewdney, July 24, 1884. RG 10, Vol. 3576, File 309 A.

_____. J. M. Rae to Edgar Dewdney, Jan. 13, 1885. RG 10, Vol. 3576, File 309 A.

_____. Hayter Reed to Superintendent General of Indian Affairs Lawrence Vankoughnet, Jan. 29, 1884. RG 10, Vol. 3774, File 36846.

_____. Hayter Reed, Jan. 26, 1888. RG 10, Vol. 3574, File 309 A.

_____. Lawrence Vankoughnet to Edgar Dewdney, July 24, 1884. RG 10, Vol. 3576, File 309 A.

_____. Lawrence Vankoughnet to Edgar Dewdney, Feb. 5, 1885. RG 10, Vol. 3576, File 309 A.

_____. Western Treaty No. 6. RG 10. Vol. 1847. File #IT 296 / I57A.

National Indian Brotherhood. "Indian Control of Indian Education." Policy Paper Presented to the Minister of Indian Affairs (Ottawa: National Indian Brotherhood, 1972).

Newhouse, David. "From the Tribal to the Modern: The Development of Modern Societies" in *Expressions in Canadian Native Studies.* Edited by Ron F. Laliberte et al (Saskatoon: University of Saskatchewan Extension Press, 2000).

Peers, Laura. *The Ojibwa of Western Canada: 1780 to 1870* (Winnipeg: University of Manitoba Press, 1994).

Pelletier, Isadore. Interview with Michael Bird, Regina, Sask., Dec. 14, 2004.

Pettipas, Katherine. *Severing the Ties that Bind* (Winnipeg: University of Manitoba Press, 1994).

Philips, Donna, Robert Troff, and Harvery Whitecalf (Eds.). *kâhtâayuk: Saskatchewan Indian Elders* (Saskatoon: Saskatchewan Indian Cultural College, 1976).

Póirtéir, Cathal. "Folk Memory and the Famine," in *The Great Irish Famine.* Edited by Cathal Póirtéir (Chester Spings, Penn.: Dufour Edition, 1995), pp. 219-231.

Preston, Richard. *Cree Narratives: Expressing the Personal Meaning of Events* (Ottawa: National Museums of Canada, 1975).

Price, Richard. "Introduction," in *Spirit and Terms of Treaties 6, 7 & 8: Alberta Indian Perspectives.* Edited by Richard Price (Edmonton: Indian Association of Alberta, 1975).

_____. *The Spirit of Alberta Indian Treaties* (Edmonton: Pica Pica Press, 1987).

Queen vs. *Big Bear*, 1885. Sessional Papers, 1886, No. 52.

Quinney, Margaret. Interview with Louis Rain, unknown location, Feb. 18, 1974. IH-202. Indian History Film Project, SIFC Library, Office of Specific Claims and Research, 1974.

Ray, Arthur, J. R. Miller, and Frank Tough. *Bounty and Benevolence: A Documentary History of Saskatchewan Treaties* (Montreal and Kingston: McGill-Queen's University Press, 2000).

Regnier, Robert. "John McLeod: First Nations Educator." Unpublished paper (Saskatoon: University of Saskatchewan, 1997).

Roan, Lazarus. Interview with Louis Rain in *The Spirit and Meaning of Treaty 6, 7, & 8.* Edited by Richard Price (Edmonton: Indian Association of Alberta, 1974).

Royal Commission on Aboriginal Peoples. "Report of the Royal Commission on Aboriginal Peoples, Vol. II: Restructuring the Relationship" (Ottawa: Canada Communications Group, 1996).

Royal Saskatchewan Museum. *mistasiniy* file (Regina, Sask.).

Sanderson, Clifford. Personal communication with author, James Smith Reserve, Aug. 17, 2003.

Saskatchewan Indian. "The Louse that Roared," Jan. 1974.

Saskatchewan Indian Cultural College. "Federation of Saskatchewan Indian Senators' Meeting," Prince Albert, Sask., Dec. 17, 1975. CD 00499.

_____. "Proposal for a New School to Serve Little Pine, Lucky Man, Poundmaker, Under the Direction of the Band Councils of Little Pine, Lucky Man, Poundmaker," Sept. 1973. From the private papers of John R. McLeod.

Saskatchewan Indian Federated College. Minutes of co-ordinators meeting, Dec. 19, 1979, p. 1.

_____. Mission Statement, 2003. www.sifc.edu/about/SIFC%20Mission%20Statement.htm

_____. *Statement of the Saskatchewan Indian Language Program, 1978.* www.sifc.edu/Indian%20Studies/IndigenousThought/fall98/language.htm

_____. "Working Mission Statement," Department of Indigenous Studies (2003). www.sifc.edu/Indian%20Studies/dept_inst.htm

School Committee Conference. Sixth Annual School Committee Conference, Sheraton-Cavalier, Saskatoon, Sask., May 1 - 2. From the private papers of John R. McLeod, 1967.

Sioui, Georges E. *For an Amerindian Autohistory: An Essay on the Foundations of a Social Ethic* (Montreal: McGill-Queen's University Press, 1992).

Sluman, Norma and Jean Goodwill. *John Tootoosis* (Winnipeg: Pemmican Press, 1984).

Smallboy, Isabel. Interview with Louis Crier and Phillip Soosay, Ermineskin Reserve, Alta.. n.d., Indian History Film Project, SIFC Library, Office of Specific Claims and Research. IH-208.

Smallboy, Robert. Interview with Abraham Burnstick, Small Boy's Camp, Alta., n.d. Indian History Film Project, SIFC Library, Office of Specific Claims and Research. IH-209.

Smith, Linda Tuhiwai. *Decolonizing Methodologies* (New York: Zed Books, 1999).

St. Germain, Jill. *A Comparison of Canadian and American Treaty-Making Policy with the Plains Indians, 1867-1877.* Master's thesis (Ottawa: School of Canadian Studies, Carlton University, 1998).

Stanley, George. *The Birth of Western Canada* (Toronto: University of Toronto Press, 1992 / 1936).

Stevenson, Winona. *Decolonizing Tribal Histories.* PhD dissertation (University of California at Berkeley, 2000).

Stick, Alex. Interview with Louis Rain, Cold Lake Reserve, Alta., Feb. 18, 1974. Indian History Film Project, SIFC Library, Office of Specific Claims and Research, 1974.

Stonechild, Blair and Bill Waiser. *Loyal till Death: Indians and the North-West Rebellion* (Calgary: Fifth House, 1997).

Stonestand, Bill. Audiotape telling the story of *pîkahin okosisa*. James Smith Reserve, Nov. 5, 1995.

_____. Interview with author, James Smith Reserve, Nov. 1996.

Taylor, John Leonard. "Canada's Northwest Indian Policy in the 1870s: Traditional Premises and Necessary Innovations," in *The Spirit of Alberta Indian Treaties*. Edited by Richard Price (Edmonton: Pica Pica Press, 1987), p. 9.

Tobias, John L. "Canada's Subjugation of the Plains Cree, 1879-1885." *Canada's Historical Review*, 64 (4), 1983: 519-48.

_____. Letter to John R. McLeod, May 2, 1973. From the private papers of John R. McLeod.

Tonkin, Elizabeth. *Narrating our Pasts: The Social Construction of Oral History* (Cambridge: Cambridge University Press, 1992).

Tootoosis, Ernest. "Culture and the Cultural College." Film. (Saskatoon: SIFC, 1975).

Tootoosis, John. Interview with Murray Dobbin, Poundmaker Reserve, Sept. 9, 1977. In *Towards a New Past*. Saskatchewan Archives Board, A1178/1179.

Tootoosis, Wilfred. Interview in *In the Words of Elders: Aboriginal Cultures in Transition*. Edited by Peter Kulchyski, Don McCaskill, and David Newhouse. (Toronto: University of Toronto Press, 1999).

Union of Saskatchewan Indians. Constitution and Minutes of Meeting, 1946.

Vandall, Burton and Jerry McLeod. Interview with author about Gabriel Vandall, World War II veteran, James Smith Reserve, April 17, 2005.

Vandall, Peter. *wâskahikaniwiyiniw-âcimowina / Stories of the House People*. Edited and translated by Freda Ahenakew (Winnipeg: University of Manitoba Press, 1987).

Vansina, Jan. *Oral Tradition as History* (Madison: University of Wisconsin Press, 1985).

Venne, Sharon. "Understanding Treaty 6: An Indigenous Perspective," in *Aboriginal and Treaty Rights in Canada*. Edited by Michael Asch (Vancouver: University of British Columbia Press, 1997), pp. 173- 207.

Vizenor, Gerald. *Manifest Manners: Postindian Warriors of Survivance* (Hanover, NH: Wesleyan University Press, 1994).

_____. "Trickster Discourse: Comic Holotropes and Language Games," in *Narrative Chance: Postmodern Discourse on Native American Indian Literatures*. Edited by Gerald Vizenor (Albuquerque: University of New Mexico Press, 1989), pp. 187-211.

_____. *Wordarrows: Indians and Whites in the New Fur Trade* (Minneapolis: University of Minnesota Press, 1978).

Waugh, Earle H. and K. Dad Prithipaul. *Native Religious Traditions* (Waterloo, Ont.: Wilfred Laurier University Press, 1979).

Weinrib, Lorraine. *Indian Treaties: An Historical Study* (n.p.: Indian Claims Commission, 1971).

Whitecalf, Sarah. *kinêhiyâwiwininaw nêhiyawêwin / The Cree language is our identity: the La Ronge lectures of Sarah Whitecalf.* Edited and translated by Freda Ahenakew and H. C. Wolfart (Winnipeg: University of Manitoba Press, 1993).

Whitehead, Josie, and Helen Whitehead. Conversation with John and Ida McLeod, James Smith Reserve, 1976.

Wolfe, Alexander. *Earth Elder Stories* (Calgary: Fifth House, 2002).

INDEX

Italicized numbers refer to photographs.

Neal McLeod's first book of poetry, *Songs to Kill a Wihtikow*, was short-listed for several Saskatchewan book awards, including Book of the Year, in 2005. Nominated again at the Anskohk McNally Aboriginal Literature Awards, it won the Poetry Book of the Year award by unanimous decision of the jurors. Another collection, *Gabriel's Beach*, is forthcoming from Hagios Press in 2008. His current research is exploring Indigenous conceptions of land and space. *Cree Narrative Memory* represents the first fruitful results of that research.

Neal is also a painter, having studied at the *Umeå Konsthögskola* (the Swedish Academy of Fine Arts at Umeå). He has exhibited work throughout Canada, including the 2005 exhibition *au fil de mes jours* at *Le Musée national des beaux-arts du Québec*: the exhibition was remounted at the Museum of Civilization in 2007. Neal was one of the founding members of the Crow Hop Café, and is currently leading the comedy troupe, the Bionic Bannock Boys, who created the film, *A Man Called Horst*, a cult classic that was screened in Berlin in 2002.